THE BUSINESS BIBLE
A 10-Step Revolutionary Guide to Conquering Your Business

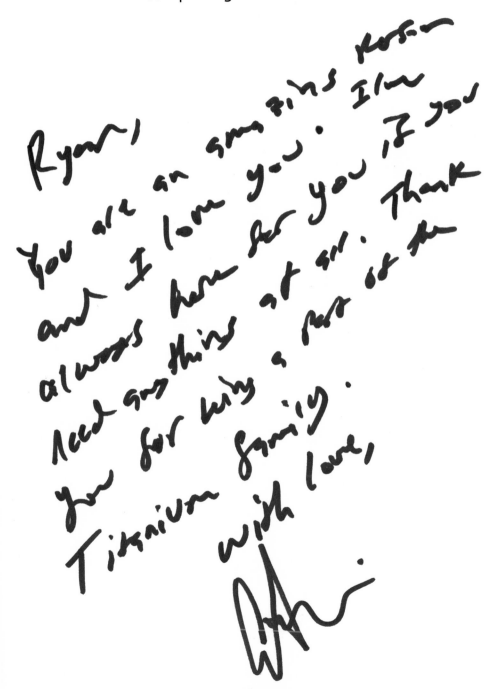

Ryan,

You are an amazing person and I love you. I'm always here for you if you need anything at all. Thank you for being a part of the Titanium family.

with love,

THE BUSINESS BIBLE

A 10-STEP REVOLUTIONARY GUIDE TO CONQUERING YOUR BUSINESS

There is science behind success in business

ARMAN SADEGHI

This book is dedicated to my family. They have stood by my side every step of the way. It is dedicated to my incredible wife, who loves me more than anyone else has ever loved me, supports me in everything that I do, and puts up with my long hours at the office. To my beautiful little girls, Ava and Sara, who sit on my lap while I work on the computer late at night and early in the morning. It is dedicated to my father, who always told me I could do anything to which I set my mind. To my mother, who showed me what it meant to work hard as she juggled two jobs for most of my life and still found time to cook, clean, and take care of us. To my mother-in-law, who has encouraged me to share my knowledge with the world for the last ten years. To my brother, Mike, who treats my children like his own and my sister, Mitra, who is an amazing role model for my wife and I. To my sisters, Angie and Ellie, who have challenged me, supported me, and guided me since our childhood. Finally, to my nephew Bijan Arman Mir, who was named after me so he inspires me to be a better man every single day.

Thank you all for making me the man I am today and thank you for your unwavering support. I love you all.

CONTENTS

Acknowledgements

This book would not be possible without the amazing people who helped bring it together.

My Most Influential Bosses:
The people who taught me about business and leadership by being great bosses and showing me what it meant to be an entrepreneur when I was still an intrepreneur working for them:

Mohammad Honarkar, my amazing mentor in business for many years and through many different businesses.

Frank Peters, the man who plucked me out of Circuit City and gave me a chance to learn business at the start of my career.

My Coaches:
The people who taught me about business, life, and how to be the best CEO and entrepreneur I could be.

Anthony Robbins, a coach like no other, who got me started on the path to be the best that I could possibly be from before I had a driver's license to this very day.

Jim Rohn, the one who taught me that in order to have more, I had to become more.

Richard Bandler, who taught me how to communicate more effectively with other people and how to influence everyone around me so they can be the best version of themselves.

Jim Collins, the man whose writings have guided me in business for the last two decades.

Ken Blanchard, who taught me about management, leadership and the art of creating raving fan employees and clients.

Richard Franzi, a business coach who not only understands business but cares so deeply for his clients that he continued to coach me for over a year, even when I was struggling so much that I could not afford to pay for his coaching.

Douglas Gfeller, a great business coach and business mind who seemed to always know the answers when I needed guidance.

My Editors:
Jennifer Peterson, the most amazing transcriptionist and editor on the planet who I could count on for support at any hour of the day on any day.

Lauren Taylor Shute, my awesome editor, a "brilliant angel, and an absolute editorial genius" who helped make this content even better.

My Design Team:
Mihai Fugulin, Sorin Codrut Cucu, Adriana Cocirta, and Adrian Mihaila, who are responsible for all of the beautiful designs on everything I create, including the beautiful cover on this book.

My Most Loyal Employees:
Gaston Wilder, a friend and colleague who has been by my side for over seven years.

Todd Mills, an amazing father, husband, and a gentleman who has been by my side in business for over seven years!

My Creator and Eternal Guide:
God, who has been there for me in the best of times and the darkest of times and has never left my side.

Introduction

Over 50% of businesses never turn a profit for the business owner.

Think about that for a moment. Most businesses fail at doing the one thing that they are intended to do. In fact, many well-meaning business owners and entrepreneurs ruin their own personal finances as a result of their business' failure.

In most cases, people pursue entrepreneurship because they find that they are good at certain aspects of business. This does not mean, however, thatthey are good at all aspects of business. The good thing is that entrepreneurs can use their strengths to make up for their lack of knowledge in other areas. For the most part, you can learn all the different aspects of running a business in order to create a thriving empire.

The reason so many businesses fail is that entrepreneurs bank on what they know and never take the time to educate themselves on the areas of the business which they do not understand. In some cases, they attempt to hire people to take care of those missing pieces, but this just leads to further complications, because it is nearly impossible to manage someone when you don't understand what they do. This is not to say that you cannot manage someone who is an expert in a particular area, because you can. Understanding the basic concepts required for that position will allow you to hire someone more knowledgeable in that field, allowing you to focus on your strengths instead.

As it turns out, learning the different aspects of running a business is actually quite simple; so simple in fact that I've been able to distill it down to ten critical areas that you need to understand and master. These ten areas are the same regardless of the type of business, and they have been consistent for many centuries, even though the specific tools used within them have changed many times. By understanding these ten different areas of business, and learning the latest and most cutting edge tools to use, you can create a thriving, profitable business that gives you the lifestyle that you deserve. Most importantly, applying these ten principles means that you will have a sustainable business built on the basic foundations that can last a lifetime, instead of a business that may work one day but fail the next. In fact, learning these skills also means that you will be able to conduct business in just about any industry or economic situation and thrive while others will falter or even fail.

The creation of these ten secrets comes from over two decades of my own personal business experience, as well as over two decades of studying the most successful business owners and entrepreneurs in the world. I started my first business before my sixteenth birthday, which means I had a business license before I even had a driver's license. And while that was my first official business, I actually had my first entrepreneurial venture without an official business license at the age of ten. In fact, it's the business that I had when I wasten that taught me much of what I know about business now.

Of course, at the time, I got some things right and I got some things wrong. But looking back, I can now see that the areas in which I succeeded were the parts of the ten secrets that I intuitively understood or was lucky enough to stumble upon. The areas where I struggled were those that I did not yet understand and, for the most part, did not learn until a decade or two later. But after starting twelve different businesses and achieving massive success as well as devastating failures, I have grown with every experience. Most importantly, because my desire for learning business is about creating systems that others can follow, I have not only tried to figure out how I can succeed, but I have focused on developing systems and tools that anyone can use to attain success in business.

It was only after years of growing and learning, failing and succeeding, trying and struggling that I was finally able to build this formula. What makes these ten steps different than any other system in the world is that everything in the Titanium Business Model considers not only the business, but also the most important asset (or liability) in the business: YOU!

Most business programs focus purely on the business and make the mistake of thinking that with the right business tools, any business can succeed. What they miss, however, is that the most important factor in any business of any size is the person at the helm. That means in order to ensure that your business thrives, it is essential to ensure that you thrive. Many people that read that statement may say that they will undoubtedly thrive once their business is thriving. But the inherent flaw in that concept is that your business will never thrive until after you learn to thrive personally.

This means that in order to develop your thriving empire, we must also develop you into a thriving individual. The beauty of this is that once you are thriving and your business is thriving, you will now feed one another consistently, and you will excel personally at an even higher level while your business thrives at levels that you cannot even imagine.

An entrepreneur is born

I have started many businesses from the ground up throughout the last twenty-three years of my life, but looking back, it was my first business that really laid the groundwork for my entire philosophy on business. Of course, I didn't know this at the time, as I was only ten years old and my business was very much unofficial, but I can certainly see myself becoming the businessman I am today during those formative years.

When I was ten years old, I wanted nothing more than to belong. My parents were immigrants and were dedicated to teaching me our culture, but as a kid in Los Angeles, all I wanted was to be cool like the other Americans. I watched the other kids from afar, searching for anything that would allow me to join their ranks, until one day I saw what I was looking for: baseball cards. All the cool kids were playing with them, and I figured that if I collected them too, they would think I was cool as well. Now, keep in mind that I was from an immigrant family, so I had absolutely no idea what baseball cards really were, but I knew that if the other kids thought they were cool, I'd better learn to like them!

The following Sunday after my discovery, I went to Price Club (now Costco) with my parents for our weekly grocery store trip. We were walking down an aisle when I saw them, the holy grail of coolness, sitting there, waiting for me to unleash their power. I picked up the box of baseball cards and felt them give me strength. I had to bring them home and make them mine. Then I saw the price tag, and my heart dropped. There was no way my parents were going to spend $33 on something just for me; we could barely afford rent, let alone something extravagant. My desperation must have shown, though, because after begging and pleading with them in the middle of Price Club, they agreed to buy them for me.

After that, I was a goner. I absolutely fell in love with baseball cards, sitting on the floor of my bedroom and spreading them out in a fan around me. At school, I asked one of my friends which was the cool card to get, and when he replied that it was the Mark McGwire rookie card, I ran home and searched through my cards for it. The box my parents bought came with thirty-six packs, each with nineteen cards. I had six hundred and eighty-four chances to get the card of my dreams, but as I opened the packs one by one, no Mark McGwire card was in sight. For the next few days, I sat around the house going through the six hundred and eighty-four cards over and over again, thinking that the magical card would somehow appear and I would at last be cool amongst my classmates. No magic happened that week; I didn't get the card I wanted, and sadly, the kids were no more impressed with me than they were before, even though I had the start of a baseball card collection.

The next week, we were going to Price Club again and I thought, "Yes! I'm going to get my parents to buy me another box of baseball cards!" We could barely afford to pay the bills, but I wanted baseball cards. We arrived at Price Club and I begged them to buy me another box. I knew if I had to, I could guilt them with my tears, and at a certain point I found myself throwing a good old-fashioned temper tantrum.

I said, "I have to have these cards!"

And my parents replied, "No! We bought you one box. We're not buying you another one. All you do is sit around all day and play with those silly things. They're useless."

In the end, they decided that paying the rent and putting food on the table was more important than buying me a box of playing cards, so I went home empty-handed.

I must have cried for hours, but looking back, that was the best thing that could have happened to me, because an entrepreneur was born that day. Back at home, I began to strategize. I certainly wasn't going to let my clueless parents ruin my chances of being cool. The box was only $33, so I would have to figure out my own way of making that money. As I dried my tears, I realized that while I was only after the Mark McGwire card, there were others who might be interested in the other cards and would be willing to trade. But trading wasn't going to work for me, because the Mark McGwire card was clearly the best card to have and anyone who had it wouldn't be willing to give it up. If I did this right, though, I could find a way to get the card of my dreams and even grow my collection in the process.

I threw all of my energy into learning as much about baseball card trading as possible, rushing through my homework so that I could devote all my time to getting that money and getting that card. I learned that there was a book called The Becket, which listed the individual value of baseball cards, but seeing as I couldn't afford the $4 to buy a copy, I borrowed one from my friend. I painstakingly wrote down all of the really valuable cards so I could look for them in my collection, and as I went through my cards, I realized that out of all of them, there were really only about twenty that I would want to keep — the rest didn't interest me. Besides, by this time, I had gotten really into it and some of the cards were for players on opposing teams, so I certainly wasn't going to be a traitor and collect their cards.

I had a lot of cards I didn't want and I needed to make money... suddenly I found myself going door-to-door to sell my baseball cards in order to get enough money to buy my next box of cards. This is when Arman the salesperson and businessman was born. I was the shyest little kid; I couldn't talk to anybody. But when I had my "why" – when I knew what I wanted and why I wanted it – suddenly I could knock on doors all day long.

Here is what I knew then that most business people don't know today: I knew that knocking on doors would mean selling cards. Selling cards would mean making money. Making money would allow me to buy another box. Buying another box would mean possibly getting the Mark McGwire card. I knew that getting the Mark McGwire card would get the kids to pay attention to me. Most importantly, I thought that that would lead to having friends and not being an outcast. Knocking on the doors of strangers is very hard to do if you're just trying to make money, but it's the easiest thing in the world when it's connected to thing you truly want most in life. For me at that time, it was having friends.

On day one, I had sales of $5 after four hours of going door-to-door selling individual baseball cards to anyone willing to buy from me. It might not seem like much now, but the way I saw it, I was over 15% of the way to my goal! After the second night, my parents were so impressed with the work ethic I had shown that I was able to convince them to invest in my company by loaning me the money to buy my second box of cards. This was a Sunday night, and I promised them that I would pay them back by Thursday if they loaned me the money. That night, they loaned me the money and I got my box of cards, but I made a deal with myself that I would not open a single pack until I paid back my parents.

The next morning, I went to school and thought about my business all day long. I came home that afternoon, and from the minute I got home to as late as I could stay out, all I did was go door-to-door. I didn't open a single pack of those new baseball cards, which is the hardest thing you could imagine for a little kid. Instead I went door-to-door selling individual baseball cards as well as packs of baseball cards, now that I had added to my catalog of products. And what do you know? A third of the way through the box, three days later, I had gotten back my $33 investment and I was able to pay my parents back.

At that point, I could have either started opening the packs and enjoying the rewards of my hard work, or I could have focused on growing my business by trying to sell enough to buy another pack. I decided my mission was to go to Price Club again on Sunday. I thought to myself that if I could just sell another $33 worth of cards, I could buy another box and keep this business going. I ended up doing just that. I worked extremely hard, overcame my fear of rejection, put up with people telling me to leave them alone, and even got over having sore feet from walking so much, but I got myself another box of baseball cards that Sunday. Most importantly, I bought this box with my own money and without help from anyone else other than my customers who had invested in what I had to offer.

As I kept pushing ahead, I made some critical business observations. For one, I realized that if I could keep my margins up and sell individual packs and cards at a high enough price, I could keep this business going forever and I could even open some packs myself in order to find my special card. I also realized that I had different "Client Groups," because while some people bought cards from me because they really liked baseball cards, others bought from me because they were just trying to be nice to the cute little boy at their doorstep. Since these were two completely different client groups with completely different needs, I decided to begin offering them different packages.

Instead of selling everyone unopened packs of cards, to some, I offered my special "ribbon" packs. These consisted of about fifteen cards, plus five bonus cards. The first fifteen were "common cards," which have zero value to a collector; I then added two five-cent cards, two ten-cent cards, and an All Star card to the top. I got these little ribbons from Target and tied them around these special packs. This was perfect because the people who collected cards or knew about them wanted the unopened packs, but the people who were buying them because I was a cute little kid actually preferred the packs with a ribbon, since they were more homemade.

My new packages were a huge hit! In fact, my cost was close to nothing on them, but the people purchasing them actually preferred them because they were created to meet their needs perfectly.

Once I identified who was interested but not a collector, I would say, "You could buy these. These are unopened; you never know what you're going to get. Then over here, there are twenty cards, and each one comes with an All Star card."

And they would say, "Oh, that's what I want," especially since the ribbon-packages were cheaper than the unopened packs.

Now I was selling packs, and I was taking the common cards that were cards I didn't want and I was selling them too! Now I could open three packs of baseball cards, keep all the cards of my favorite players for myself, and the other two packs of common cards people would buy from me. It worked for them and it worked for me.

I later created a third group of clients who I considered "advanced collectors." For these folks, I had something completely different. I invested in some binders with sheet protectors and put the cards in there. I even bought myself a little price tag gun. I got the new edition of the Beckett each month and priced my best cards inside of the notebooks for those interested in buying specific cards. Of course, I priced the cards above the Beckett price since I was offering my services door-to-door. Now when I knocked on someone's door who was a baseball card enthusiast, they would sit there and go through my notebook and buy individual cards from me. Sometimes I'd sell one single card for $25. That's almost enough for an entire box! It was an incredible experience, and while it was not a real business, it was my first taste of having a business.

Every single day, I went door-to-door doing this, but after a while, I realized that I couldn't do this alone if I was going to grow my baseball card empire. I decided it was time to hire some employees. There was a kid who lived in my neighborhood who had a little brother, so I recruited both of them to come work for me. The first time I had these kids go knock on doors, they completely froze.

The older brother stepped up to the door and looked back at me when the door opened and said, "I don't know what to say. What do I say?" all while the potential customer looked at us, wondering what was happening.

This is when my first "sales script" was born. It was difficult for them to follow the script at first, so I role-played with them, having them knock on my door fifty times to deliver their script until they could do it as well as I could. This is why I love business – it just makes sense. The tools I use to run my businesses today are no different than the basic tools I needed to run my "business" then. What works in business is mostly common sense. Unfortunately, most business owners do not tap into their common sense, so they spend their entire career thinking there is something magical about success in business when it's really just a matter of applying some simple, common sense principles.

I taught these kids their sales scripts and got them to overcome their fear of rejection, and suddenly the two brothers were working for me and selling for me. They were making money and I was getting additional revenue and profits as well. Of course, there was no risk in it for them, so they were happy, and I was okay with taking the risk by buying the cards up-front since I knew we'd get the results I wanted. Before I knew it, I was going to Price Club every Sunday and we could get one, two, or even three boxes of cards. But things suddenly started to turn.

Unfortunately, these trends didn't last forever. If you're in the donut business and you love donuts, you have to be careful that you don't eat too much of your profit. Well, I really liked baseball cards, so at one point, I got too excited and opened too many of the packs, and one week I found myself not being able to afford to buy any more boxes of cards. This is when I learned the importance of reading a balance sheet and knowing how much inventory you have. But it was amazing; I created an amazing baseball card collection, which still I have to this day, and I got my Mark McGwire rookie card! I got everything I wanted and created notebooks and notebooks full of cards in the process.

Business is simple. We make it complicated, though, because we forget what business is all about. We forget that business is about figuring out how to deliver a certain product or service that people want. If you understand why you're doing it in the first place, all you've got to do is market the business, sell your product or service, have some systems in place, and offer a few different packages to specific client groups, along with a few other things I'm going to share with you later in this book.

The following year, my family moved to a house where we had a garage on a street that got some traffic. I started up the baseball card business again, but this time as a retail shop instead of going door-to-door. I even came up with some amazing marketing systems to get my clients to come back again and again.

I remember taking the Mark McGwire rookie card and photocopying it, which you're probably not allowed to do. I blew it up to the size of a full sheet of paper. I didn't have a computer, so I cut out letters from a newspaper to make a sign, and with this I created "specials of the day." I am in shock when I think back, but I actually had different specials each day and I went through hours of work to create new flyers, but I always wanted to make sure I had something new to catch people's eye. One day, I would offer a certain brand on sale, and another day I would offer certain packages, but I always had something new and different to get people in and keep them coming back.

Then I created something that most businesses to this day do not do a good job of doing. When people came to visit my retail location (my parents' garage), I gave them a reason to come back the next day. I don't know where I came up with this idea at such a young age, but I decided to give every customer a photocopy of a random card after they purchased anything from me. I'd hand them the photocopy and tell them to make sure they stopped by the next day because I would have a new "card of the day" featured, and if their photocopied card matched the card of the day hanging on the garage door, they would get a free pack of cards!

I now had every kid in the neighborhood stopping by my house each day to check to see if they'd won. After school, the kids would gather around my driveway and other kids who lived further away would convince their moms to drive them down. We even had random people stop by to see what was going on since there were so many people standing around. It was amazing that by giving a few packs of baseball cards away each day, I was able to get the kids to come back over and over again. Of course, each time they came, most of them would inevitably buy something else, so the system more than paid for itself.

Imagine if I could give one pack away but sell three packs in the process; while that means I'm essentially discounting my overall sales by 25%, it makes perfect business sense for a business that operates on 50% margin. That's still a pretty darn good margin! Some people don't do that. Whatever business you are in, these are the kinds of things you've got to think about. You've got to stop having your head so far in the business that you are not thinking outside of the box everyday and about how you can take your business to the next level.

Sometimes you have to get up and look at your business and say, "What am I not doing that would be super simple? How can I get people to come back to my business? How can I get people to buy more? How can I add more value? How can I offer a package that is a better fit for a specific group? How can I simplify my business? How can I invest more in my business? How can I do something no competitor is doing?" If I hadn't asked myself those questions, my first business wouldn't have been nearly as successful, and I likely wouldn't have learned from the experience as much as I did.

This is the time for your mind to start going, so you can spend the rest of this book reading with your conscious mind while your subconscious mind is spinning away and finding ways to revolutionize your business and your industry. I tell you this story not only for you to see where my crazy business brain comes from, but for you to see how every business comes from a place of necessity. I needed those baseball cards. It wasn't about the money. When you make business about business or you make business about money, you fail. There are very few people in this world who are truly motivated by money. There may be a very small percentage of people who are actually motivated by money, but most are motivated by other things. The exception you sometimes find are those who have lived through something like the Great Depression. If you remember the Great Depression or had a parent who experienced it and really drilled it into you, you may actually be motivated by money, because to you, it means survival. That's not the case for most of us, though, nor should it be.

Most of us aren't programmed to be driven by money. We've got to stop thinking about business as being about money and instead find out why we're in business in the first place. It is things like this that lead me down the path of personal development and business coaching. I have studied business and business people extensively. I have studied their psychology and their driving force. I have realized that businesses thrive when the person at the top of the company is thriving personally. If I, as an individual, am thriving, I can make my business thrive. If you are a doctor, you need to be thriving personally before you can help your patients thrive. If you're a lawyer or a real estate agent, you need to be thriving if you are going to represent your clients best. If you're a CEO, whatever you may be, you must thrive as an individual if your business is going to thrive. Once I had people surrounding my garage eager to hear what I had to say, I thrived too, and my business absolutely soared.

From baseball cards to CEO

I've had quite an interesting journey since the days of my baseball card "business." The content you will find in this book comes from twenty-five years of real business experience, mixed with some very unusual experiences that most business owners do not have. Everything I share with you in this book comes from pure science, mixed with the reality of what actually works in the real world.

At around the age of fifteen, when the computer revolution was just starting to take off, I fell in love with the idea of personal computers. At the time, the internet was not something that people were using yet, and things such as email didn't exist except for a few government institutions and a handful of schools that used it for various purposes. It was at this stage in my life that I started my first real business. I saw an opportunity to set up internal networks for various companies. Doctors and lawyers were amazed when a letter typed up on their secretary's computer could magically be brought up on their computer for editing, and then sent back without having to carry a floppy disk back and forth. This "magic" was the start of the technology that now powers the internet, but it was unknown to most at that time. As an early adopter, I was able to help companies revolutionize their industries by incorporating technology into their businesses. Today, I find myself doing much of the same and I see business owners having the same types of objections and internal conflicts. In fact, when business owners object to some of the new technologies I talk to them about today, it is a reminder of those who told me they would never have a need for email and that a "car phone" was designed to be in a car and not carried around in our pockets.

Within a short period of time, I was doing so well financially that I was able to move out of my parents' house and into my own two-bedroom apartment, which was much more than I needed. I purchased my dream car and was living the life that I had always thought I wanted. At this point I was associating with mostly adults; I rarely hung out with people my own age since I felt so out of place with them. I didn't want to talk about normal high school stuff; I wanted to talk about business and things that my peers weren't concerned with. It was at this stage that I dropped out of high school in order to pursue my business passions full-time. Over the next several years, I grew this business and started a few more until finally deciding that I wanted to go back to school and earn an education.

Over the next several years, I studied business, biology, chemistry, physics, mathematics, and after falling in love with the science of how the human mind works, I graduated from the University of California, Berkeley, with a degree in molecular and cell biology and an emphasis in neurobiology. Several years later, I attended Harvard Medical School for about two years, but eventually I left Boston in pursuit of new entrepreneurial ventures.

Throughout this journey, I've owned businesses in multiple sectors that were completely unrelated. I have owned restaurants, night clubs, a business consulting company, training companies, IT companies, recycling companies, marketing companies, photography and videography businesses, and just about everything else in between. All in all, I have started somewhere around twelve different companies and I am proud that most of them have succeeded. But others have failed miserably, and this book is as much a product of my business failures as it is a product of my successes. Every time I have failed, I've come out stronger and more prepared to take on the next challenge. Failure, after all, only leads to growth if you treat it the right way.

Today as I write this book, I own six different companies. Of those six companies, most are in completely different sectors and have nothing to do with each other. Chances are, my experiences withthese twelve different companies have somehow touched most of the aspects of your business. Considering the fact that, today, one of my businesses has over one hundred and fifty employees and multiple large warehouses, trucks, and operations in addition to all the basics of sales, marketing, and everything else, I can certainly connect with anyone who has businesses in either manufacturing or logistics. One of my companies is an online retailer, so I have vast experiences in this niche as well. One of my companies is a local small business specializing in photography and videography services, so if you have a small business that has a local presence, I understand a lot about what you do on a daily basis. Another one of my companies is a large marketing firm where we do truly revolutionary marketing, website building, search engine optimization, email marketing, PR, and everything else that goes along with allowing companies to absolutely thrive through incredible marketing. This company has a large team of people throughout the United States and an even larger group of full-time employees with various expertise throughout the world. Finally, my passion company allows me to put on incredible seminars and coachbusiness people so that they too can have successes beyond their wildest imagination.

Whatever industry you are in, the systems and skills I teach in this book will help you take your business to heights you never thought possible. In fact, if you study and follow these ten secrets, you should be able to double your profits in the next six months, and after that, you'll have a business that will thrive and grow consistently.

Take this journey with me as I share with you some of the most cutting-edge and advanced techniques in growing a business, along with some classic business concepts that have been around for centuries. I am honored to have the privilege of serving you with the ideasin this book and I thank you for joining me on this journey.

How would a neuroscientist run your business?

As you read this book, you will be astounded and excited to learn incredibly powerful tools that can help any business massively expand its profits and grow beyond your wildest dreams. While some of these tools are classic business skills that have been taught throughout the ages, many are tools that I created as a result of my unique background that combines business with neuroscience.

If you recall, my background is in neuroscience. I have a degree in molecular and cell biology and neurobiology, and I enjoy the way neuroscience is involved in just about every aspect of life, especially in business. Understanding how the human mind works is vital to a successful business, since being able to predict how and why people behave the way they do will fuel your sales, marketing, operations, and finances, and will help you understand your own mindset as a business owner as well as the thoughts of your customers and employees.

As you're reading these chapters, every once in awhile, think about how a neuroscientist might possibly approach your business. But if you forget this section completely and focus just on the business tools without even thinking about the neuroscience behind them, you'll still get valuable lessons that will fuel your business. I designed these tools in such a way that, whether you understand how they work or not, they will still get you the results.

Read this book in an alert state and focus on consistently applying the things that you learn from each chapter starting that day and going forward. Do not wait until you finish the book before you begin to implement the things that you have learned. And most of all, prepare for your business and your life to change forever.

Chapter I

The CEO Behind the Business

The first thing to understand is that the most important aspect of any business will always be the mindset of the leader. As such, you are the most important part of your company. That means you will need to focus on the many aspects of yourself as a CEO and entrepreneur. This starts with knowing exactly why you are in this particular business, understanding the role you play within your organization, what your strengths are, and where you may have blind spots that need to be filled.

Once you recognize who you are in your business and exactly why you go into it to begin with, it is critical to be completely connected with your goals for this business and have a solid exit strategy in place, even if you think you never want to sell your business. Having all of these pieces together is going to allow you to thrive in your business in a way that most can only dream of doing.

Let's go on a journey together to discover the woman or man behind the business, so we can help you take your business to new heights.

Why did you get into business anyway?

Why are you in business, or why do you want to get into business?

When I ask the question of why, I am not looking for the answer on the surface, but a much deeper answer that comes from the gut and your heart. For an individual to perform at optimal levels, he or she must be completely connected with not just what they want, but why they want it.

In your case, you must take the effort to understand why you are interested in entrepreneurship and business ownership. Some would claim that they got into business because they want to make more money. But money is never truly the why. When you look deeper, you understand that people who want more money want it for many different reasons. Some high-level executives that I have coached have told me that they started their first business because they wanted freedom. After we both chuckle a bit, they have gone on to tell me that they quickly discovered owning a business was the farthest thing from attaining freedom. But it gave them a sense of thrill and variety unlike anything else they've ever experienced in their lives.

In fact, many entrepreneurs lose interest in their business when the thrill, excitement, and uncertainty is replaced with growth, consistency, and profits. It is in these observations that I realized people operate businesses for many different reasons. In speaking with the most successful business owners in the world, I realized that they had one thing in common: when I asked them why they were in business, they did not tell me what business they were in and they did not tell me what they wanted to accomplish with their business. Instead, in almost every case, they gave me an emotional answer that came directly from the heart and spoke to the basic human needs that drive us all.

In many cases, the most successful business owners I have studied gave me stories from their childhood that inspired and drove them to achieve greatness. Often they tell stories of their failures in life and in business and how what they do today is a result of those massive failures earlier in their careers. But in every case, it was simple to see that the driving force behind them as CEO came not from the mind, but purely from the heart.

If you want to have a good business that functions well and turns consistent profits, skip this chapter and start reading from Chapter 2, because the tools shared in this book, when implemented, will ensure sustainable success for any organization. However, if you strive for greatness and want to have a business that revolutionizes your industry and even the world, while giving you consistent fulfillment and a sense of being that goes well beyond any profit and loss statement, then focus on reading and understanding this chapter.

In reality, upon completing Chapter 1 of this book, you could simply put this book on your shelf and it is very likely that you will see significantly better results in your business without learning any of the tools offered in the rest of the book. The most important and influential factor within your business, and by far the most valuable asset, is and always will be you.

So why are you in business? Why do you want the title of President, CEO, or Chairman? Why do you want to own a business? Why specifically do you want to own *this* business? What will you have if you achieve all of your goals in this business? If we wave the magic wand and gave you all of the things you've ever wanted to accomplish in your business, how will you feel? What specifically would you feel and what would you do with that feeling?

Take a few moments to focus on that concept and get connected with exactly why you are in business, and specifically, why you are in *this* business.

Resource: If you need some assistance getting more connected to why you got in this business, download the "Titanium Life" App and there are some useful audio files that can help you get more focused on various things. One of those is a closed-eye process for getting focused on why you are in this business.

Who are you in your business?

Once you know why you are in business and you therefore understand your driving force on a deeper level, it is now time to understand who you are within your business. When you look at a broad range of CEOs, presidents, or chairmen of a company, you can quickly see that the titles given to individuals rarely reflect what they actually do and their secrets to helping the business thrive. Some entrepreneurs and business owners have a title like Founder. Some refer to themselves as the CEO, president, or in some cases, the Chairman of the Board.

In reality, these titles mean little when defining who the individual actually is and what purpose they serve within the business. It's important to understand what you actually do for your company, and more importantly, what you do not do. Your duties will change what type of leader you are; in fact, while I will refer to you, the person at the helm, as

CEO throughout this book regardless of the title you use on a day-to-day basis, there are actually three types of CEOs. I use the title of CEO regardless of the fact that you may or may not be the CEO of the company, because even if you are a high-ranking executive within your organization, the key to maximum success is to think of yourself as a CEO. Therefore, throughout this book, we will simply refer to you as CEO.

The three types of CEO are entrepreneur, manager/operator, and artist/technician. The word *entrepreneur* is often generically used to talk about those who start a business, but in reality, individuals who start businesses are rarely entrepreneurs. You see, the founder of a company or the CEO might be an entrepreneur, but they may also be an artist/technician or a manager/operator. While most individuals have some aspects of all three roles living inside of them, you'll always have one that is dominant in your business, a second one that you can adapt to and learn with persistence, and a third one that can potentially be learned but is not who you are in your nature. It's critical that you find an individual to fill that gap for you within the high ranks of your organization. As you read through the next several paragraphs, notice what you are and what you are not; attempt to see who you truly are when you are in your natural state.

The Entrepreneur

The entrepreneur is the leader who enjoys taking risks. This person pushes the envelope of what is possible within a business, and is focused on growth, innovation, and reaching the maximal potential at all costs. The key here is the phrase "at all costs." You see, that's what separates the entrepreneur from the artist/technician and the operator/manager. The entrepreneur sees the business as just that: a business. While entrepreneurs can have many things that drive them and multiple reasons why they start and grow a business, the key with an entrepreneur is that he or she is focused on growing a business no matter what it takes. The typical entrepreneur will take risks that artists and operators would never dare take. He or she will be focused on the growth of the business above all else. Entrepreneurs are often the ones who push their business to be the biggest or most innovative within their industry.

The Operator/Manager

The primary focus of the operator is typically on systems, sustainability, organization, teams, management, and controlled growth. The operator is interested in seeing the business function as a unit and seeing a business grow in a manner that will be sustainable in the long haul. Operators often spend time creating or overseeing the creation of standard operating procedures that organize various aspects of a business. Additionally, operators are hesitant to make changes that are not systemic and do not consider all aspects that relate to that change.

The Artist/Technician

The artist is the one who is consumed by doing things the right way and ensuring the highest possible quality of work in the business. Artists are obsessed with ensuring that the products or services delivered by the organization are impeccable. He or she will spend hours and even years to overcome even the slightest flaws in the recipe of the business. The artist is focused on growth only as long as the quality and consistency of the results delivered can be maintained.

While all three have advantages, each also carries negative qualities. The artist/technician often stays true to the art for too long at the risk of customers not being interested in the product being offered. They limit themselves in the marketplace to only those who agree with them and their style of doing things. Additionally, artists rarely build procedures that others can easily follow because they see what they do as an art form that cannot be replaced with a system. While the artist is the one who allows the business to thrive early in the lifecycle, he or she is also the one who often impedes the growth of the company.

The operator often stays the course for too long, and in the case of many large companies that control their sector one day and are bankrupt the next, it is almost always the operators at the top of the company who felt they could keep the business going in exactly the same way and did not see the changing of the tides. Or, perhaps they saw the change and because there wasn't enough entrepreneurship at the top, they did not recognize or feel the need to make drastic changes.

Entrepreneurs are the ones who people credit for most of the businesses that take off, but in reality, entrepreneurs are far and few between and are not necessarily the most successful ones in the business world. While some entrepreneurs do succeed, many spend most of their careers growing businesses and then watching them quickly crash because they pushed the envelope too far, spent too much money, and took too much risk.

Regardless of what you are at the core, to succeed, you must surround yourself with at least one or more people who bring the missing pieces to the table. Once you have successfully hired or partnered with the missing pieces, the key is to truly treat them like a confidant or partner, instead of as an employee. Allow them to rein you in from time to time so you are not always running the business your way but rather in the most intelligent way.

In the end, the answer is not that you should abandon whatever your natural self is and change to something else. In reality, the CEO, president, or person at the top of a company is going to have a small piece of all three of these styles with them. Everyone is an entrepreneur, operator, or artist/technician. But everyone favors one of those three, second one that is medium in terms of development, and a third one that is often quite undeveloped. The most successful CEOs in the world are those who know and embrace what they are best at, while also acknowledging and understanding the piece they have the least of inside of them.

If you are an artist and lack the entrepreneur, then perhaps you can find an entrepreneur that can come into your business and help you push the limits and meet the demands of the customer, even when those demands don't directly meet your art. Perhaps you are an operator and you need to bring on that artist or entrepreneur who contributes the missing piece. Either way, regardless of what you are at your core, find the piece that you have the least of and bring that individual into your organization. Work to develop the parts of you that are less developed so that you can be more of a well-rounded CEO.

What is your dream with this business?

When was the last time you thought about the reason you're in business? What is your dream with this business and where do you intend on taking it? I'm not quite talking about your exit strategy just yet; that will come up later. But for now, I want to know where you want your business to go. How much growth do you foresee having in the next 12 months? Three years? Five years? Ten years and beyond?

What is your dream in terms of the products and services you want to provide? What kind of revenues do you want to have? What kinds of profit? How many employees do you want to have? How many offices or branches? Do you see yourself as being involved in the day-to-day on a regular basis or is your goal to sit on the board of your company and allow others to run it?

In order to find ultimate success in your business, it's important to remind yourself of exactly where you want to head. It is very difficult to get yourself to where you want to be if you don't exactly know where it is that you want to be. Focus on taking just a few minutes to write down your ultimate vision for your company. Document what you do what you do and where you see the business going. Once you know where you want to be with your business, take some time to think about how that will make you feel and what that will give you. Is it freedom you are after? Is it financial abundance? It is power? Significance? Certainty? Is it the fact that you will be able to contribute immensely to the people you love and even people you don't know? Is it just one big challenge that causes you to grow and that's why you're in business?

We all have different reasons for being in business. While many of us share some of the same factors, it is critical to get connected with where you see yourself going with this company and what your ultimate goals are within this business. It's important to get as specific as you possibly can by using numbers, metrics, facts, figures, and anything you can document on a piece of paper or a computer. It is those reminders that will keep you going when the days get long, the economy takes a turn, and the times get tough.

Take the time to capture exactly where you want to get with your business and then focus on how it will make you feel to be there. It is then that you will have that rocket fuel to push yourself to an even higher level and to get you through those tougher days.

What is your exit strategy?

People start businesses for many different reasons and we all have different ideas of where we see ourselves at the end of the road. Now that you have a basic idea of where you want to see your business go, it's time to think of your exit strategy. I know that some of you are building a business and you have no plan of ever exiting it. But that in itself is an exit strategy, because if you plan on keeping a business for a lifetime, you are planning on exiting the business on the day you leave this planet. You better make sure that you set things up correctly or your business will soon follow you.

For most people, an exit strategy will be something along the lines of how big they want to grow the company and how they want to make an exit from a financial perspective. Let's consider some different exit strategy options.

EXIT STRATEGY

Establish and sell

In this model, you establish a business quickly, creating the systems, procedures, and establishing some sort of market share with an incredibly powerful idea behind your concept so you can sell the business to someone else - most likely a competitor who will want to purchase you to get the systems you have developed.

Build, grow, and sell

In this model, you are entering the business with the idea of creating the business, getting everything together, and then growing your revenues and profits to the point where the company is financially stable and has built enough credibility that someone will be interested in purchasing the company from you. This is typically a multi-year plan and is usually focused much more on establishing greater than the previous model. In order to maintain a viable business to sell later, you must establish sustainable profitability. As opposed to the previous model, whereas you have the concepts in place, someone may be interested in paying you for your business.

Grow and take public

In this option, your goal is to establish a business and grow it so that you can take the company public. Taking the company public can of course bring with it significant financial gains, but there is a lot that has to be done in order for this to happen. It is very valuable to know ifyou plan to take your business public as early in the game as possible, so you can establish the systems and procedures that will create an ideal scenario for you.

Create a lifestyle business

In this model, you are getting into business and growing it in order to generate revenue with sustainable profits, with maximal focus on simplifying the systems and procedures in order to have the least amount of pressure on you, while still maintaining profitability. In this business model, the key is you want to create a business that allows you to travel and enjoy time off with friends and family, without being overburdened with a significant number of things that are going to take you away from the things you love.

Grow and hold

In the grow and hold model, you are establishing a business with the idea that you are going to grow the business. While you are not necessarily looking for a lifestyle business that allows you to take long vacations, long weekends, and times where you can work from a laptop on a beach for months on end, you are instead looking for a business that you can work in on a consistent basis similar to a 9-to-5 job with no intention of ever going public, selling the company, or significantly reducing your hours.

Family legacy model

In this case, you are building a business that can be handed off to family members, often your children. You are in business with the idea that you can grow the business and establish systems that will allow you to pass the business on to your family. In some cases, you have already identified the family members to whom you would like to pass the business. In other cases, you may not even have even have kids yet. But you have thought that you care about your business so much and you are so passionate about it that you see yourself doing it for a good portion of your life before passing it on to others in your family, with the hopes that the business and its legacy will long outlive you as an individual.

While these are some of the most common exit strategies, there are many more and there are combinations of these that can be employed. The key for you is to pick one of these or create your own exit strategy. Make sure you know exactly where you are going with your business, because, once again, it is hard to get to where you want to be if you don't know where you are trying to go. Take some time and document your exit strategy. Keep in mind that your exit strategy and your vision for the company can change at any given time, but at least if you should have some sort of a documented exit strategy, you're not flying blindly.

Once you have a concept for your exit strategy, try to place as many numbers, facts, and figures on it as you possibly can. For example, if you plan on selling your company, document some facts and figures about exactly how big you want your company to be and how much you want to sell it for if you plan on taking it public. Consider what valuation you want your company to have the day it goes public. If you are going to have a lifestyle business, consider how many hours you want to eventually work and how much profit you want to have with that schedule. Focus on documenting as many details as possible so you can make this incredible dream of yours a reality.

Chapter II

Bottle the Essence of Your Business

When I ask most business people what business they are in, they typically give me some generic answer that involves the name of some industry. For example, people tell me they're in residential real estate, the fashion industry, photography, or marketing. But rarely do people actually tell me what business they're in.

When someone asks you what business you're in, what they are trying to find out is what you provide. So if you are in real estate and some asks what business you're in, it might be that you're really in the business of making people's dreams come true by helping them find the home of their dreams. Do you see how that is quite different than being in residential real estate?

Now when you think of someone saying, "I am in the business of making people's dreams come true by helping them find their dream home," you might think that that sounds like something you would say in an elevator pitch so you can sell more houses. But notice what it does for you emotionally when you consider that the person makes people's dreams come true as opposed to simply being "in residential real estate." You automatically connect more with the person who makes people's dreams come true, and understand what they do on a more personal level, thus possibly providing them with a new advocate for their business.

One of the keys to be as successful as possible in your business is to know exactly what business you're in, which involves knowing what it is that you offer your clients and how you solve their pain points.

What business are you in?

As a business owner, it's critical to take a step back and think about what business you are really in. Most of us are so busy trying to get new clients, manage expenses, and deliver results for our clients that we often forget to take that step back and think about what we are really doing.

To understand this, let's take a bit of a theoretical approach. Let's think about what the purpose of a for-profit business is and how that plays into everything within society and the world as a whole. The purpose of a for-profit entity is to provide some goods or services in trade for money. But what is money? Money is simply a way for members of our society to compensate one another for the value that has been added. In essence, the more value you add to society, the more you are financially compensated for it. Not to say that every form of adding value to society gives you financial compensation, but certainly if you are adding value, you can be compensated for it if you so choose.

If the purpose of a business is to make money and the way to earn money is to add value, then it makes sense to think that in order to grow your business and attain massive levels of success and profitability, you must add more value – more than you have been adding and greater value than anyone else in your industry adds. But how do you add more value? That is the question that will get to the roots of what business you are actually in. If you think about the way that you add value to society, regardless of what kind of a business you have, you will quickly realize that your business is actually a lot more exciting, interesting, and valuable than you thought previously.

For example, if you think you're in the shoe business because you have a retail store that sells shoes, that sounds quite boring and not motivating to most people. But if you think of yourself of being in the business of allowing women to be fashionable and comfortable while expressing their identity with the shoes that they wear on the weekends, now you have something that you can really work towards that adds more value to society. I know that some of you may not be very excited by that last sentence, but that's okay. That's why you're not in the women's shoe business.

If you sell insurance, you could think of yourself as being in the insurance business, or you can think of yourself as being in the business of helping business owners protect the assets they have worked so hard to build. You do this by giving them exactly the right amount of coverage for their needs, so they do not overspend but have complete protection. Once again, if that doesn't excite you, that's why you're not in the insurance business.

Think of what value you are adding to society. Whether you do Business-to-Business(B2B) or Business to Consumer(B2C), it does not matter. The only reason your business exists is to add value to society. Think of how you are adding value to society and you'll figure out what business you are in. By going through this exercise, I am certain that as you're reading this book, you are already starting to become more excited about your business and about what you do. It is because of these minor changes in the way that we look at our businesses that allows us to thrive and beat the competition. It's these little things that get us up an hour earlier than our competitors and keep us a bit more focused while we're at the office. It is these small distinctions, such as focusing on the value you add to society, that will help you thrive while others struggle.

What end result do you deliver your clients?

So now that we understand this idea conceptually, let's go through an exercise where we figure out exactly what it is that you do. To start, let's think much more broadly. Let's think about how you are going to answer the question "What do you do," focusing on the value you add to society. Consider these two critical things:

1. What gets you excited, and would get you out of bed and into the office an hour earlier every day? This is the part that will appeal to you and get you motivated and excited about your business.

2. If someone who was in your ideal client category asked you in an elevator or at a conference what you do, what answer would very quickly get them thinking, "Wow, that's exactly what I want?"

(i) What answer would get them to identify themselves as the type of client you provide your services for?

(ii) Does your product or service address one of their key pain points?

(iii) Do you provide a product or service that no one else does?

To review then, there are two parts: one about you, and one about your ideal client. The part about your ideal client is divided into three subsections. Think of all these things as you consider what you do. To help you come up with some answers, I've listed a few examples, but don't think that yours have to sound just like the examples, because we are all different. The purpose of the answer to "What do you do?" is that it should get your heart excited about the value you are adding to society. For example:

- **Commercial real estate**: "I help successful business owners find a space where their team can grow and develop, while also creating an investment in the future of their business and their families."
- **Hair salon**: "I help people feel beautiful and have the self-confidence they deserve so they can accomplish even more."

Once you have come up with this, you will have the answer to the question of "What do you do?" And if you do it right, it will appeal to both you and your ideal client. Notice that every one of the examples above gets you excited about the business. And if you happen to be one of the ideal clients, notice that it would be hard to leave that elevator without asking more questions. In fact, I know that's what most of you are thinking. You are thinking, "Well, in most of these cases, the people don't know what I actually do" and that's the question they asked you.

You are correct. While we have answered part of their question, we have not really answered the entire thing. But notice that we have said enough to get ourselves excited, and more importantly, get our ideal client extremely excited and intrigued. The follow-up question that your ideal client will almost always ask is, "How exactly do you do that?"

How exactly do you do that?

Typically, when you tell someone what you do in the format I just explained, if they are one of your ideal clients, they will almost always ask you, "How exactly do you do that?" But even if they don't, you can still tell them by saying something along the lines of, "And I do that by..."

When they ask you how exactly you do that, you can now dig deeper and be more specific by telling them exactly what products or services you provide. So if you are in the shoe business, you can now say, "I do that by having an awesome retail store in the mall, where women can come in and browse through some of the latest fashions with the help of my amazing customer service team." For the case of someone in commercial real estate, they can now say, "I do that by helping business owners find the perfect building for their business and making sure that they get the best possible price, so their building is an investment in their future and not a burden."

Unfortunately, most people when asked what they do, instead of answering in the first way I explained, they quickly jump to answering the question of how exactly they do that. While this makes the conversation flow a bit easier, it unfortunately does not help your ideal client identify themselves as such. Additionally, it does not get them or you excited about your business. But now that we have taken step one and established the excitement, and they have identified themselves as your ideal client or perhaps someone they know as your ideal client. Now you can tell them exactly how you do it, so they have the specifics.

Take a moment to answer both of these questions in writing, and make sure that you have a solid answer that flows well and is one that you can repeat easily.

1. What do you do?
2. How exactly do you do that?

By answering these questions, you are head and shoulders above your competitors, because most of them have no clue what they do. If you have salespeople or just about any kind of employee in your company, you are going to want them to learn to say this statement as well. The only difference is that they might put a bit of their own job or title into this. If they work in your warehouse, for example, they will put something additional into the second part of the statement that lets people know they are part of a warehouse team. But the end result is that everyone in your organization should be focused on saying things that ignite massive interest from your ideal clients and also creates excitement within them and everyone with whom they speak.

What makes you better than the competition?

I am really excited at this point about the fact that you finally know exactly what you do and exactly how you do it. And by taking the statement above and using it in every interaction about business, you are going to instantaneously see interest in your business increase in a way you've never imagined. You will start to find that your ideal clients will find you, instead of you constantly trying to find them, and they will identify themselves as such, regardless of where they meet you – even if it is through an online blog post or someone else talking about you. Soon, everyone will know you as the person who does that thing you said you do, instead of what they used to know you asbefore, which was what industry you were in.

What I want you to understand at this stage is that the most valuable thing you have done is to identify that you are nothing like the competition. There are tens of thousands of people in the United States who are in "the real estate business." But how many people do you know who are in the business of making people's dreams come true by helping them find their dream home? Notice that by doing this, you have essentially eliminated 98% or more of the competition and you are now doing business in a realm that others are simply not in. You have gone from being in a crowded space to suddenly being fairly lonely at the top. But I don't think that's such a bad thing.

Now that you're there, we're going to take it one step further and think about what makes you different and better than the competition. It is important for you to make a list of every way in which you are different and better; this list is going to turn into the ammunition and tools you have around your belt. During any sales presentation or any point where you are trying to tell someone about your business, it is critical for you to be able to differentiate yourself in any way you possibly can. It is these differentiators, as small as they may seem, that will tell people how you are so much better than the competition.

Here are some examples of differentiators:

1. At Nordstrom, they do a lot of things better than the competition, but one thing that is simple and costs them nothing is the one that is the most important in my mind. Nordstrom employees are trained that they should not hand the customer their shopping bag across the counter. Instead, they walk around and hand it to them. Simple. Nothing more. But this small act is a differentiator that defines the entire culture for customer service at Nordstrom.

2. My friend and client, Amy Sims, a real estate agent in South Orange County, California, purchased a moving truck and now allows anyone involved in a real estate transaction with her to use

her moving truck free of charge just for doing business with her. Again, not too many real estate agents are doing this.

3. Titanium Success. Even in my own company, I had a moment onstage last year when I made a decision that has forever changed what I do. I decided that all of my main events for Titanium Success would be "name your own price," with people being able to attend for as little as $1. I did this not because there is some gimmick where we can magically make money off of someone who pays a dollar to come in. There are no tricks or secrets where we swindle additional money out of them. It is purely because the content that I deliver is revolutionary and I don't want anyone to miss out on the opportunity. I can tell you for a fact that absolutely no one else in the personal development industry is doing this.

4. A salesperson at a wireless store I used to coach took my teachings and did something that was more successful than any other campaign this store had ever run. He went to the store and bought a bag of Tootsie Rolls. He wrote some nice comments on small strips of paperthat he cut and taped to the Tootsie Rolls. The message on the paper said, "I want to thank you for doing business with me, and I don't have the means of doing much more than this, but I hope this small gesture shows you just how much I appreciate that you are my customer." He gave a Tootsie Roll to every person who bought a phone from him. The key was that he would not give Tootsie Rolls to anyone other than those who purchased a phone from him.

More so than anything else, it was what he said when he handed over the Tootsie Roll that made all the difference. He would say, "This is a small gesture to show you just how much I appreciate the fact that you've done business with me, and I want you to know that over 60% of my sales come from referrals. If you appreciate the quality of service I've delivered you, I ask if you could please tell two or three of your friends about me and tell them to call me personally on my cell phone so I can help them with whatever they need. Even if they are not in the market for a new phone, I'm happy to help them solve any technical issues they may be having or help answer questions for them, even if they are with a different carrier." With that simple act, this man became one of the top salespeople in the entire country.

Notice that all of the things listed above are extremely simple but are differentiators that make you different and better than your competition. While some of these can cost significant amounts of money, there are many things that are absolutely free. The key is for you to identify what you are going to do to set yourself completely apart from the competition, then make a list of all those things and make sure that you and your team are consistently doing those things.

Keep in mind that your competitors will quickly catch on to what you are doing and you will have a lot of copycats, which is a good thing. This is because it shows that you are powerful and are headed in the right direction. But as you'll learn in Chapter 11 of this book, you must constantly innovate, which means that whatever is your differentiator today will not be the same one a year from now. You must constantly be focusing on what the next thing is that you can do to help you be even better than the competition, even as they grow and attempt to copy you.

Here's a quick step-by-step approach to making sure you are ready to move to the next stage:

1. Think about your business and the value you want to add to society.
2. Document what you do.
3. Document how you do it.
4. Make a list of all the ways you can differentiate yourself from the competition.

By doing all of these things, you will put yourself in a place where you literally have no competition, and that is exactly where you want to be.

Chapter III

Identify Your Ideal Client

The first step to starting or growing any business is knowing exactly who you are going to attempt to help with your products and services. The keyword here is *exactly*. Your goal is to identify your ideal customer so that everything within your business is built to ensure two things:

1. It attracts your ideal customer or client.
2. It absolutely does not scare away or disenfranchise your ideal client.

That may seem like a very simple concept but when you break it down, you'll realize that so much of what we do in business is done blindly and for the masses. We run the risk of doing things that do not attract our ideal client and, much more importantly, we sometimes do things that push away our ideal clients. Whether you are just a startup or you've been in business for two decades, it's time to establish your ideal client and then go back and analyze every aspect of your business to make sure that it speaks to your ideal client.

Things as simple as your logo, the color scheme you use on your brochures, the design of your website, your company tagline, and even your company name should all be designed to keep the two rules above in line. Imagine if you had a beautiful logo, a high-end website, or a great company message that everyone loved, but there was some aspect of it that pushed away your ideal client.

I see this everyday with clients I coach in business. Over 80% of the businesses I coach do not know who their ideal client is and have never taken the time to determine their ideal client. Even worse, I see 95% of those who don't bring me in for coaching making these same mistakes. Those are the ones who seem to think they've got it figured out.

In order to succeed in business at the highest possible level, it is important to understand exactly who your potential customers or clients are. This is not to say that you have to limit your products or services and only offer things that a small subsection of society or the business world may be interested in. Instead, it's a simple realization that in order to properly create the best products and services and to market them effectively and inexpensively, you must have very targeted areas of focus. By consistently focusing on the exact type of client you are trying to target with each product or service that you offer, you are able to do several powerful things in one.

Stop trying to be everything to everyone

No product or service is going to be exactly the same for everyone. Let's use a man named Torrance as an example. Torrance owns and operates a small gym, and is trying to bring in more clients. He currently tries to attract anyone interested in health and fitness, and since his service offerings include personal trainers to help people achieve maximum results, Torrance has no choice but to hire personal trainers who are incredibly diverse so that they appeal to everyone who goes to his gym. The problem is that these trainers are not extremely specialized, and of course, very expensive for him to employ. Because he's not tailoring his services, he now has to offer subpar service to essentially everyone who walks in the door.

The reason for this is very simple. One potential target group for a gym would be fitness competitors. If a gym is going to focus on fitness competitors, it is clear to see that many things about that gym are going to need to be different, including the type of trainers employed, the variety of supplements and additional items offered for sale at the cash register, and even the décor on the wall.

I remember walking into a gym in San Diego, California several years ago and I noticed the images of body builders like Arnold Schwarzenegger blanketing the walls. At the time, I was very focused on having a world-class body, and it was inspiring to see so many champions and the work they had accomplished. At the same time, images of Arnold Schwarzenegger may not be exactly what attracts a forty-seven-year-old mother of three who has gained weight after all of her pregnancies and now would like to shed twenty-five pounds by joining a gym. Additionally, it would be clear to see that the type of personal trainer that it would take to train a future bodybuilder is completely different than the person who is going to train someone who is looking to lose a few pounds and gain some strength. So, in trying to appeal to everyone, Torrance appeals to no one.

Tailor your marketing

It's easy to see that the methods and message used to market to Sally, thestay-at-home mom, will be totally different than the methods, message, and the placement of ads used to market to Jericho, the body builder. As we will discuss later in the marketing chapter of this book, you can substantially reduce your marketing costs while massively increasing the results you get by creating campaigns with razor-sharp focus.

Customize your sales process

Again, the methods, tactics, tools, settings, features, and benefits used to sell to Jericho will be completely different than what will be used to sell to Sally. Now, the best salespeople in the world have the ability to quickly adjust their presentation and offerings to match the needs of the client. The reality is that people like that are very few and far between, and even they are more effective when they can stay focused on one type of sale with one customer demographic. Just because you as the business owner have the ability to quickly adjust the features and benefits you offer in order to convince both Sally and Jericho to sign up at your gym does not mean that you are going to be able to hire a salesperson who can do that as well.

Customize customer service and relationship building

Even once you have established someone as a client, it is much more difficult to satisfy vastly diverse groups of people than if you were focused on a specific subset. An example of this, of course, can be as simple as the decorations that hang on the walls of a gym or the messaging on your employees' uniforms, and even the various methods you use for bill collection.

The fact of the matter is most businesses try to be everything to everyone. One of the first questions I ask business owners and executives is "Who is your ideal client?" I am always shocked by the fact that most business owners have no clue who their ideal client is. But of course, that is not what they say. When I ask them about their ideal client, I always get an answer. The answer is almost always the same thing, just phrased differently by different people. That infamous answer is: "Well, anybody."

I'm not sure why this surprises me, considering the fact that I had no clue who my ideal client was for most of the businesses I started in the first half of my career as an entrepreneur. Interestingly, in a few of the businesses, I got lucky and naturally developed a following of a specific type of client. Even though I kicked and screamed to try to appeal to everyone, I was unable to do so. This was possibly the biggest blessing I could have had.

Trying to be everything to everyone is simply not a tactic that works. It is usually at this point in the conversation that business owners will tell me that they actually do have an ideal client group and I get excited, put a smile on my face, and ask them to tell me who that ideal client group is. Unfortunately, when they tell me, again, it is almost the same answer every time: "Well, we are sort of everything to everyone," but said in a different way.

For example, a business owner who had a fashion line with surf gear said that histarget was people who were interested in surfing or surf gear. That may seem like a perfectly good answer, considering he had a brand that soldfashionable surfing gear. But I want you to understand that that is essentially saying that he wants to be everything to everyone. After about an hour of coaching, we came to the agreement that his ideal client was actually something much more specific than he had thought previously:

1. Males
2. Age 16-22
3. Hardcore surfers
4. Fashionable
5. Popular or those who want to be popular within the surfing scene
6. From families whose household income is $100,000 or more

Notice that this is a very different group than just saying, "People who are into surfing." Now does that mean that they did not sell female surfing gear? No. In fact, they had quite a large selection of surfing gear for women. But by understanding that females were not his ideal client or that young men who were twenty-five or four-teen years old were not his ideal client, or that those whose family's household income is not at least $100,000, he was able to create every aspect of his company in a way that directly appealed to his ideal client.

We were able to absolutely ensure that he would never alienate his ideal client while still capturing as much of all of his other audience sectors as possible. Do not try to be everything to everyone. Decide exactly who your perfect or ideal client is, and then build your systems so that they appeal to them and make sure that you never put anything out that would alienate them.

Create customer groups or market segments

For businesses that have multiple services, especially those that are very different, you could potentially have multiple ideal clients. But before you start creating too many market segments and too many groups of ideal clients, keep in mind that the more you do this, the more diluted your message will become to your actual ideal clients from whom you probably gain the majority of your profit. But if you do indeed have multiple products and services that are vastly different, you may need to have multiple ideal client groups.

Once you have identified exactly who your ideal client is, you can create all of the market segments to which you wish to market. This is now where the person who owns a surf line can acknowledge the fact that he would like to market some of his products to younger kids who are still in high school, are not driving yet, or even to teenage girls. Yet a completely different segment such as men in their thirties and forties could also be targeted. In fact, he could even launch a line for skateboarders, snowboarders, or other groups like that.

But the key is that each of these different market segments is going to be created independently and with specific details in mind. For example, we mentioned that in his case, his ideal audience might have ranged in age from sixteen to twenty-two years old. But then we said he could add a second segment that was from twelve to six-teen years old, and a third one from twenty-two to twenty-eight years old. The temptation here will be to say, "Then that means his audience ranges in age from twelve to twenty-eight years old." But that is not at all the case, because the messaging and other marketing will be completely different for each age segment.

More importantly, as we are segmenting these different groups, we are going to slice and dice them in different ways. For example, while the household income of the kids from six-teen to twenty-two needed to be over $100,000, that may not be the case for the folks between twenty-two and twenty-eight years old, because we may assume that they are now on their own and don't have as much money to spend. Even if they only make $30,000 a year, though, they may find surf fashion important enough that they are willing to make an investment in it. In this case, their family's income is irrelevant to their spending habits, and they still might be part of this client group.

All of the examples I'm giving here relate to a business-to-consumer company (B2C), but all of these rules apply for business-to-business (B2B) as well. In fact, when you're thinking about B2B, you have to consider not only the demographics of the company, but also the people who are in the roles you are trying to target. The end result is that you want a very specific target audience with multiple different market segments that are clearly defined in writing so you can navigate effectively and deliberately.

While it is critical to establish your ideal client type and be sure to know absolutely everything you can about them, it is equally important to have other potential client groups to whom you can market and provide your products and services. While your product and service might be best for your ideal client group, there are almost always additional segments of the market to whom you can have your product or service appeal.

For the most part, these additional market segments are not groups to whom you try to appeal on a broad level, but instead you appeal to them in targeted marketing campaigns. That means you should not focus on trying to brand your company in a manner that is everything to everyone. Instead, you should create branding that appeals directly to your ideal client group and then focus on creating marketing that allows you to target additional groups with the proper messaging. You can also consider adding additional products and services that will appeal to these additional groups. But all of your efforts with these groups must be focused on ensuring that you never alienate your ideal client.

Today, with targeted advertisements through social media and other channels, it is very easy to target various groups with specific messages and images that appeal directly to them. So while your company's branding as a whole can appeal to your ideal client, you can easily attract additional groups of potential customers.

The $100,000 Lead Test

At this point, you should have an idea of who you think your ideal client is. But for eight out of ten entrepreneurs that I coach, I know that even at this point they are still holding on to the idea of everyone being their ideal client. Knowing that money tends to get people thinking in the right way sometimes, I use what I call the $100,000 Lead Test to see if you have truly honed in on your ideal client. So let's put your ideal client to the test.

Step 1:

I am going to charge you $100,000 to get 100,000 of your ideal clients into a stadium. That means that you are going to pay one dollar per person. If you are in B2B, these would be the people at the ideal client business types you are looking to target. So, knowing that you are going to pay for every single one of those leads to be in that stadium, my question is: Are you still okay with the ideal client that you have? Or are you thinking you may want to put some more restrictions on who you're willing to pay to have in there?Here are some examples to get you thinking in the right direction:

B2C(Business-to-Consumer)

For B2C, is there an ideal gender for your ideal client? Ideal age range? Interests? Hobbies? Salary range? Net worth? Location? Are they renting or owning a home? Being able to answer these questions is key to identifying your ideal client.

B2B (Business-to-Business)

If you offer your products or services to other businesses, then answer some of the questions from the B2C section above. But most importantly, focus on the types of businesses you would do business with. Consider things like geography, type of business, number of employees, and annual revenue.

Answering these simple questions about your ideal client can help you identify exactly who you are most interested in targeting through your marketing, as well as to whom you are going to develop your products and services to serve the best.

As a side note, as you are thinking about getting up onstage and talking to these 100,000 people, you may consider what you are going to say so that you can keep them in the stadium to hear you speak; because, as you will learn in the next chapter on marketing, these people have not eaten all morning and you are going to be speaking during their lunch break. So if the first thirtyseconds of what you say does not compel them to want to stay, you will have spent $100,000 with nothing to show for it. Between now and the marketing chapter, you may want to think about that. Do you have your ideal client yet?

Step 2:

I am not convinced that you are at your ideal client yet, so I am going to change the rules of the game a bit. Instead of 100,000 people at a dollar apiece, I am instead going to give you 10,000 people, but you are now paying $10 per lead. So the question is: At $10 per lead, are you still willing to stick with the same group or are you interested in honing in a bit more on who your ideal client is? What age ranges or geographies would you eliminate? What interests or hobbies would you now demand? What income or revenue would now be mandatory for you to be willing to get them into that room? Answer these questions and you will have identified your ideal client. Then be sure to pick up the other groups you may have left along the way by creating anywhere from two to five additional ideal client groups.

Step 3:

Once again, I am not convinced that you have your ideal client, so we are now going to raise the price to $100 per person and I am only giving you 1,000 leads. Remember, you are making a $100,000 investment and I am only putting 1,000 people in front of you. Don't throw your money away just because you want to keep a broad audience. Instead, remember that you can capture a lot of other groups as part of your second, third, fourth, and fifth market segments. But the purpose of the ideal client is to identify exactly who you are going to target.

Step 4:

I know you worked really hard in the last step, and as much as you didn't want to, you created a more targeted ideal client group, and I am very proud of you for that. But I'm still not convinced, so I'm going to have to raise your price yet again. This time, I am going to be charging you $1,000 per person and I will only be putting a total of 100 people in the room with you. How does this change your idea of the ideal client? Consider that there are only enough seats for 100 people in that room and you are paying $1,000 per person, so any seat that you give up is not just costing you $1,000; it's costing you one additional space in the room, because now you are only limited to 100 leads.

Think carefully about how this affects the type of people you want in the room. If you are B2C, consider making your target age range smaller, seeing if you should focus on one gender over the other, see if income should play a bigger part in your ideal client selection, and if you should be more picky about geography or interests. For B2B, consider if you should hone in more on companies based on size, revenues, profit, geography, number of locations, industries, or any other factors.

Step 5:

Wow, that was very impressive! It seems to me like $1,000 per person was the magic number, that finally got you to understand what an ideal client group truly is. It looks like you have honed in on your ideal client quite well. And if you are doing this exercise along with me, you are starting to see how much better it feels when you start to realize that you don't have to be everything to everyone. I can bet that you feel a sense of relief inside of you, knowing that you don't have to think that everyone is your ideal client.

Considering how good it feels, I want to give you one more gift. I am raising the price on you yet again. I am now giving you only 10 leads, and each lead is going to cost you $10,000. Depending on how well you did in the last round, you may or may not have a lot of room to move at this point. But I want you to see if there are any additional adjustments you would like to make, considering that you now have only 10 seats in the room, and each seat is costing you $10,000.

If that's the case, what are the requirements you want in place before we get those people in the room? Are you sure you don't want to eliminate some companies further based on size or geography? Are you sure you don't want to change your requirements for age, interests, or income? Think about it very carefully, as you are about to invest $100,000 of your hard-earned money to get 10 people in front of you.

If you have done this exercise, then I can guarantee that you have an ideal client group that you are ready to base your entire business around. If you are just starting your business, build it to serve these people. While you can include other market segments, don't forget: these are the people you want to build everything around. Don't worry about being everything to everyone, because believe it or not, others will still listen to your message. But the more you target everything by focusing on your ideal client group, the more your message will be consistent and the more likely you will be to attract more new clients.

Get specific with your market segments

Starting with your ideal client group and then working your way to your other market segments, it is time to document specifically who your client groups are. There are some great tools available to help you do this, and the best thing is that,while they are designed to sell you advertising, you can actually use them without buying the advertisement.

If you have a Twitter or Facebook account, simply go to their advertisement section and start placing an ad. In Facebook's Ad Manager, for example, you will have the opportunity to select your ideal client group based on many different lists. Go through this process in either Twitter or Facebook and select your ideal clients based on all of the different categories available. Think of all the things we mentioned in the previous chapters, including age, gender, income, net worth, number of employees, revenues, profits, geography, and just about anything else that is listed there, including hobbies, interests, groups, and even the magazines that a person reads.

Once you have gone through this process and created the group, you do not have to hit 'next' and purchase advertisement. You could simply document the things you selected and that will become the profile for your ideal client. Then proceed to your other groups by changing the criteria, broadening things, or simply creating additional market segments based on completely different criteria. Be sure to go through this process for every one of your ideal client groups and market segments so that you do not have to play a guessing game the next time you are looking to place an ad or the next time you write an article. Instead, you and everyone on your team will always know exactly who your ideal client is.

There are other tools available that will allow you to do this further, including sites like LinkedIn, which may give you additional options when it comes to companies and job titles. Whatever tools you use, the key is to document every aspect of your different market segments in as much detail as possible. Once you have done this, you will have an idea of who you are marketing to. As you go to the next chapter on marketing, think about how much easier your job is now that you know exactly who your ideal client is.

Imagine going through the next chapter of this book without knowing who your ideal client is and trying to be everything to everyone. When you think about that, you will realize why most companies, including possibly yours in the past, have struggled significantly with creating a marketing message. It is almost impossible to have a message when you are trying to be everything to everyone.

Chapter IV

Become the Known Expert in Your Industry

Building exceptional marketing systems allows your business to bring in qualified leads on a consistent basis. This not only allows you to have more leads, leading to more sales, but it also allows your business to tap into new sales channels that you cannot possibly reach with sales alone. The most successful businesses in the world have extremely large marketing budgets because they understand the importance of getting qualified clients to find them, instead of always doing it the other way around.

Without marketing, you are at the mercy of your sales reps making cold calls or your current clients giving you referrals. Inject marketing into this scenario, however, and you will find yourself in a place where in addition to all of the other ways in which you receive qualified leads, you will now have qualified leads identifying themselves as your potential client and finding you. When done well, marketing can certainly be the boost your business needs.

Unfortunately, over 90% of marketing budgets for small companies are wasted on things that never even pay for themselves. That means that over 90% of all marketing budgets, including advertisements and PR, result in a negative return on investment (ROI). If 90% of small business' marketing budgets are completely wasted, then how is marketing such a powerful tool? The power of marketing comes in knowing exactly where, when, and how to spend marketing dollars and how to track them to ensure that you have a significantly positive return on investment.

With the right marketing system in place and analysis tools that allow you to analyze ROI on a regular basis, you will be able to create a perpetual marketing machine. A perpetual marketing machine is one in which money goes in one end and profits come out the other end. If the profits (not sales) are higher than the amount that has gone in, you can simply take a portion of the profits and add them to your marketing budget for the next month. This will increase your marketing budget, which can theoretically increase your profits even more, which will then allow you to pump even more money into marketing.

When done properly, a perpetual marketing machine can be built to propel a company to be many orders of magnitudes larger in a short period of time. This is what is typically seen in the rise of some of the biggest companies in the world, such as Microsoft, Google, Apple, and Facebook. But be careful how you spend your marketing dollars, because the world of marketing has been turned completely upside-down over the last decade.

Traditional marketing is dead

Make no mistake about it: the old methods of marketing are completely dead. Advertisement in newspapers, magazines, television, radio, and other things popular throughout the 20th century are almost completely dead. That does not mean a Super Bowl ad is not the right move for Pepsi or Budweiser. But it does mean that for a small business, over 99% of the traditional marketing avenues available will yield almost nothing.

When business owners hear that the old methods of marketing are dead, they immediately think then that must mean I'm referring to the fact that the new method of marketing is done entirely on the internet. This is when they typically get a big smile on their face and tell me that I shouldn't worry, because they are spending almost their entire budget doing online marketing. It's at this point that I unfortunately have to tell them that online marketing done the traditional way is dead as well.

Unfortunately, over 80% of online marketing budgets are used as if the internet is nothing more than a television or newspaper. With the amount of information that is coming at people today, it is impossible to hold their attention long enough with your advertisement to actually make a difference, especially if your advertisement or marketing piece is targeted towards a general audience.

So what has changed to kill traditional marketing?

The biggest change in our society today is the massive amount of information that is coming at each of us on a daily basis. Because we are all constantly in a state of information overload, things that used to capture our attention can no longer do so. Additionally, we live in a world where we are lazier than we've ever been in the past. It used to be that an average person had at least thirty phone numbers memorized. Today, most of us barely even know our own phone number. That means that when we watch television, the information we see does not necessarily translate into us taking action, because it requires us to remember to do something in an era where there is very little we have to remember. Our smartphones, emails, and calendar systems sync across platforms and are able to remind us of everythingwe need to know; why add something else to the list?

Additionally, most people simply do not read newspapers and magazines like they used to; therefore, the demand for content in print has decreased. With this decrease, you would assume that the cost of advertising through these channels would have also decreased. But unfortunately, this is not the case. In many cases, the cost of advertising in newspapers, magazines, radio, and television has actually increased because these outlets are desperate for survival and must do whatever they can to keep their heads above water. Therefore, they have great sales teams who go out and attempt to sell their products and services, all for a marked-up rate in order for the company to make a profit.

Sadly, many companies are still utilizing these avenues thinking that a big, colorful ad in a local magazine is actually going to drive business traffic to their company. There are very rare cases where, for specific types of businesses, this is true. But for most cases, that is not reality. Today, there is only one type of marketing that works, and the beauty is that it is so eloquent that it works better than any system that has been used in the past. This incredible marketing system is called educational marketing, and it is the wave that has taken overevery industry. While it has been around for centuries and popular for over a decade, if you are able to use cutting edge methods for educational marketing, you will be head and shoulders aboveyour competition.

From hunter to hunted: Make leads chase *you*

The concept of educational marketing is very simple. Instead of talking *at* people about yourself and your product, you focus on your potential clients' pain points and then provide them with information and education in a way that will help them overcome those problems. As you read that sentence, you can see why educational marketing is so much more effective than traditional marketing and advertising. Not only does educational marketing allow you to reach potential clients that you would have never been able to reach in the past, but it also provides you with a type of marketing that will help you retain clients and get you referrals. I'll give you an example to show how this works.

<u>Business Case</u>: ABC Solar, a business that sells solar panels

Jim is a salesperson for ABC Solar. The way he used to sell wasby knocking on doors and asking people if they would consider installing solar panels on their house. There were a variety of ways this was done and various gimmicks and tricks used. But the main gist was simply knocking on doors and trying to sell the product.

Using the concepts taught in this chapter, Jim changed his focus and instead wrote a simple one-page article called *Ten Ways to Make Your Home More Energy Efficient and Save Money in the Process.* Starting that day, instead of knocking on doors and selling solar panels, Jim would pull out his guide and tell the person who answers the door that he wanted to share a quick checklist with them that they could use to save money in their house and also become more energy efficient.

He would use a script along these lines: "Hi, today we are in your neighborhood and going to all the homes to share with them this simple guide of how you can make your home more energy efficient and actually save money in the process. There are ten different things on this list that you can do that will save you money over the next two years. However, one of those things is something that will actually start saving you money from the first month that it's done, and that is installing solar panels on your house. I work for a company that installs these solar panels. Please look at this guide and consider implementing the ten different things it suggests, because they will all be very helpful. The other thing that we're able to do is we will be going around the neighborhood tomorrow between the hours of 1:00 and 5:00 p.m., conducting free energy audits. If you're interested, I still have a few slots open and I can put your name on the list. As part of the energy audit, someone will come to your home and do a 25-point energy inspection of your home, after which you will receive a report with the findings and some suggestions. Again, we are not able to provide you with most of the things that will come up on the audit, but if you choose to install solar panels, we would love to help you with that. Is there a time between 1:00 to 5:00 p.m. tomorrow that would be better for you for conducting an audit?"

As you can see in the above example, the salesperson is providing free educational content and even offering a free inspection, instead of trying to sell the product. Multiple times during the presentation, the salesperson mentions that he offers solar panels and that he would like to sell them. But he is not there purely for the purpose of selling solar panels; he's there to educate the client as well. There are dozens of different ways to do this, and it is something you can do in every industry. But the key is to understand educational marketing and how it works.

The other beauty of educational marketing is that by creating educational content and making it available in the marketplace, you are leaving breadcrumbs everywhere that can be found by others by chance. For example, this ten-point energy checklist could be placed on a website, posted as a blog, handed out door-to-door as well as at homeowners association meetings, and might even be published in a local newspaper or magazine – not as an advertisement, but as an article that helps homeowners at no cost to you.

If you give someone a flyer or postcard that sells your solar panel services, it is very likely that within the first five minutes, it will end up in the trash. However, an energy efficiency checklist is something that just might end up on the kitchen counter or even put on the refrigerator with a magnet. In this case, not only will the homeowner not forget about you, but anyone who visits their home may also see that checklist with the company's name on it.

While you do make it very clear on your educational content what you do and how people can get a hold of you, the content doesn't feel like an advertisement. It also gives you the ability to reach out to individuals you would not otherwise be able to reach and allows you to continue to influence them without constantly bombarding them with your advertisement. Instead of feeling as though they are being used, your client feels as though they have gained something from their interaction with you, thus putting you and your company in a positive light and increasing the chances of them using your services after all.

The Stadium Pitch

I'm sure you have heard of an elevator pitch. This is something sales coaches teach in order to make sure that an individual always has a prepared pitch they can use on the spot. The reason it's called an elevator pitch is because it should be something that you can quickly say when someone asks you, "What do you do?" in an elevator before you get to the next floor. This means it must be preciseyet informativeenough so that your target audience will potentially take an interest in what you tell them you do.

While the elevator pitch is certainly better than not having a prepared pitch at all, it is not the most valuable tool you can have inyour belt. Now that you have learned the concept of educational marketing and learned why it is so incredibly important to educate instead of constantly selling or advertising, let's talk about how this relates to what we will now refer to as "The Stadium Pitch."

The Stadium Pitch is something that one of my favorite business coaches of all time, Chet Holmes, used to talk about. Sadly, Chet Holmes passed away a few years ago,well before his time. But as many of the greatest people of all time have done, he left an incredible legacy of teachings for businesses all around the world to utilize. The concept of the Stadium Pitch is very simple: instead of thinking of an elevator used to talk to one person, imagine that we allow you to make that same pitch to an entire stadium full of people.

At first you may think to yourself, *what difference does it make?Why would being in a stadium be any different than talking to one person?* In reality, you are right. The Stadium Pitch is exactly the same pitch you should use when talking to someone in an elevator. But by thinking in terms of a stadium full of people, it allows you to create a much more intelligent pitch, especially when you consider educational marketing.

First, let's lay down the ground rules. You are about to walk onto the stage and talk to a stadium full of 100,000 of your ideal or potential clients. That means whatever your service or product offerings, the individuals or businesses represented in this stadium are exactly who you would want as your customers.

Unfortunately, there are a few things we have working against you:

1. These people have been sitting in the stadium all day, starting at 7:00 a.m., and you are going to be onstage in five minutes at exactly at 11:45 p.m. Just before you come onstage, the audience will be told that there is a free buffet with lobster and filet set up outside, along with a beautiful chocolate fountain and an open bar. However, for those who choose to skip the buffet, they can stay in the stadium and listen to you give a thirty-minute presentation on your topic.

2. The individuals cannot walk out until they hear the first thirty seconds of your talk. But once they hear the first thirty seconds, they can walk out and go to the buffet if they wish. In fact, at any point during your thirty minutes, if they would like, they can walk out. Your goal is to figure out how to, first, get them to choose to stay and skip the incredible buffet, even though they are hungry and tired, and, second, how to keep their attention for thirty minutes so that you have an opportunity to possibly sell your product or service.

With that in mind, consider what the first words out of your mouth might be when you get up to speak. Because for most of the people in the room, your first words just may be your last. One thing to consider before deciding what to say is to know that for just about any product or service, over 90% of people are not currently interested. Whether you are a real estate agent, a shoe salesman, or you install solar panels, over 90% of the individuals or companies you come across are not currently interested in your product or service. In fact, only 2% of the population is looking for any typical product or service at any given time.

That means of the people who walk into a mall, only 2% or less are interested in a new pair of shoes. Elevator pitches are perfect for that 2%, because if someone is looking for a pair of shoes, a real estate agent, or whatever service you offer, they will hear your elevator pitch, get excited, smile, and ask for your business card. Unfortunately, the other 98% will not be interested, and will walk out of the elevator and never talk to you again.

In a stadium full of 100,000 of your ideal clients, we would hate to have 98% walk out. So how can we possibly keep them in the room to listen to you? The key is that you must do a few things:

1. You must speak about a topic that is much broader than your specific niche. That means if you sell shoes, you are going to have to pick a topic that is more in line with things such as fashion, foot hygiene, how the right shoes can make you more productive, or something along those lines.

2. You must present your information in the form of pure education, instead of a sales pitch at all. For the most part, there is no need to talk about what you can sell them. Instead, the focus should be on what you can teach them or what you can share with them.

3. Your topic must be engaging and focus on solving one or more of the pain points that your ideal clients have.

By following these rules, there's no guarantee that every single person will stay in the room. But research shows that doing this correctly can keep 70% or more of the audience in the room and engaged. Why? Simply because they feel that missing out on the opportunity to hear what you have to share would be a much bigger loss than the lobster and filetwaiting for them outside.

Here are some examples of stadium pitches that work, versus those that do not:

What do you do?

> **Cold**: "I'm a book editor."
> **Warm**: "I help writers develop their manuscripts so they can get published."
> **Hot**: "I help people create a lasting legacy."
> **Former Pitch**: "I am an editor and today I'm here to tell you about how the right editor can help you publish an amazing book."
> **Stadium Pitch**: "As human beings, we have a finite amount of time to spend on this planet and this is a fact we cannot change. One day, we will all be gone and the only thing we'll leave behind is our legacy. Today, I'm here to talk to you about the most significant way you can create a legacy that will last long after we are all gone."

Cold: "We do SEO."
Warm: "We help companies get to the top of Google's rankings."
Hot: "We help business owners do what they love instead of having to always focus on finding new clients."
Former Pitch: "I am here to talk to you about how you can increase your Google rankings and get to the top of search engine results."
Stadium Pitch: "As a business owner, the last thing you want is to be a slave to your business. More importantly, you don't want to have to constantly spend your time begging people to do business with you. Today, I'm here to tell you the five secrets to getting leads coming to you on a daily basis."

From expert to hero

From a very young age, as we begin to go to school, we learn who the experts are, who is in charge, and who has authority. In school, the teacher teaches and the students listen and learn. Undoubtedly, the teacher is viewed as the authority figure in the room and he or she is seen as being more knowledgeable, more experienced, and seems to have mythical and mystical powers that the rest of the individuals in the room simply do not have. While in first and second grade, this is certainly true.

As we get older and enter higher education, including college and beyond, many times the professor knows the specific topic better than anyone in the room. Often, he or she is not a mythical figure and lacks overarching powers. Yet after decades of practice, nearly everyone in the room recognizes them as the authority and somewhat of a hero. It is something that is ingrained in all of us: when someone teaches us something, we instantly see them as being an authority and some kind of a mystical creature.

As a business owner, you must capitalize on this. By practicing educational marketing on a consistent basis, you will establish yourself as an expert within your industry. When you write articles, blogs, give talks, and share your knowledge with people from the perspective of educating them instead of selling to them, you are instantly lifted to a higher level. Almost immediately, they will see you as an authority figure. Within moments of hearing you speak, 80% of people in a room will begin to respect you in a way that you could not have attained with even the longest of resumes.

In fact, many times people don't even need to listen to you speak or read something you've written. Simply seeing your name underneath the title of an article is enough for your potential clients to view you as an expert. Individuals and companies alike are constantly looking for those who can give them expert advice and opinions, and once they find those people, they prefer to buy things from them.

Even in a restaurant, we will often ask a waiter what he or she thinks is good on the menu. Often, people order the things that they recommend. This is primarily because we see them as an expert in this particular area and we know that they have knowledge about that food which we simply do not have. We ask their opinion and often listen.

Establish yourself as the expert in your industry who is called upon to speak at conferences or to write about important events happening. Now, be very careful; the goal is not to be an authority amongst industry insiders. There are many places where I see people giving talks simply educating their competitors and other industry leaders. Your goal is to speak at the conferences which your potential clients attend and to write articles in publications which your potential clients read.

While it feels great to be an expert among your peers, it will never give you any business. But the moment you speak about an important topic in front of your potential clients, you are seen as an authority, and therefore much more likely to get their business.

Write a book

If you are now convinced that establishing yourself as an authority and an expert in your industry is one of the best ways to massively increase the amount of business you can get, let's now talk about the number one way you can instantaneously establish yourself as an expert: write a book.

When I first say that to crowds of people in any industry, I typically see confused and blank stares and I know exactly what is going through their minds. Here are the excuses I typically hear:

1. I am not a good writer.
2. I don't really have enough knowledge to write a book on a subject.
3. I don't have the time.
4. There are already so many great books on this topic.

5. I don't want to be in the book writing business and I don't need to make money from writing my book.

So let's take a moment and address each of these excuses one by one.

1. I am not a good writer.

Not a problem! You do not need to be a great writer or even a good writer to be the author of a book. You simply need to know a lot about your subject and hire experts to help you compile your information into a book. There are plenty of incredibly talented editors you can hire, who have a masterful grasp of the English language and can take your simple words and turn them into beautiful sentences that flow just as well as things written by your favorite authors. In fact, you do not even have to write anything at all, because as you will hear in a moment, most of your book should be "written" using an audio recording device. All you have to know how to do is speak, and you don't even need to be that good at speaking, since if you hire an editor, they'll be the one to clean up your book. You could also hire a ghostwriter to take your material and write the book for you. Either way, you just need to be able to talk about a topic in order to author a book. In fact, you can download the Titanium Book Writing App which guides you through the entire process and makes writing a book easier than riding a bike.

2. I don't really have enough knowledge to write a book on a subject.

Not all books revolve around having the deep, thick science or facts behind things. Some of the best books in the world are written by real people about real situations that they know a lot about. For example, if you are a real estate agent in the Dallas, Texas area, I can guarantee that you can write an incredibly useful book on either real estate in general or a book about navigating the Dallas real estate market in 2016.

You may not have as many facts and figures as some of the other books that are out there. Also, your thoughts may not be as well worked out or documented as the people who write books for a living. However, I can guarantee you that your book will contain insights that real people looking to buy real properties will appreciate much more than all of the facts and figures in the other books. But if you really like facts and figures, you can either look them up and include them in your book, or after you have finished writing the basics of your book, you can pay someone to get the facts and figures for you. The bottom line is that you possess more than enough knowledge to write an incredible book. And if you don't, perhaps you should not be in the business that you are in.

3. I don't have the time.

I love it when people tell me they don't have enough time. At this point, I typically let them know that I am running seven different businesses, I put on seminars, I write multiple blogs, I have two small toddlers at home, I have date night with my wife at least twice a week, and I still had time to write a book. The reason I am able to do all of this is that I am able to use my time efficiently, and I want to teach you to do the same. You are absolutely right; most adults with real jobs cannot possibly sit at a computer to write out an entire book. But consider that most Americans drive an average of tenor more hours per week. Even if you only drive five hours per week, that is five hours per week you could be using to write your book. At that rate, you can write a book in under thirty days. All you have to do is use my simple book writing technique, which you can get by either downloading the Titanium Life App or going to titaniumsuccess. com/writeabook. Following this simple five-step approach will allow you to write a book without ever having to get on a computer or take time out of your normal day.

4. There are already so many great books on this topic.

It doesn't matter how many books are written already on the topic. The key is that you have not written a book on this topic. The only book that matters in terms of establishing you as an expert within your industry is a book that you personally write. So don't waste your time going to the bookstore to look at the books that are there and don't waste your time looking on Amazon to find a niche for which there isn't already a book. It does not matter. Unless there is a book out there with your name on it as the author, we are still one book short within your industry. Besides, everyone has something to contribute. Figure out what makes you unique, what you know that others can learn from, and focus your book on that. Create a book of value on your subject and people will be tearing down your door to learn more.

5. I don't want to be in the book writing business and I don't need to make money from writing my book.

Good! The purpose of this book is not to be in the book writing business, and the purpose of this book is certainly not to get you to sell your books. In fact, this book is very likely to be something that breaks even at best and may even cost you more money than it will ever get back. The point of this book is not to make revenue from it directly. The only purpose of this book is to establish you as an expert. Even if you only print one copy of the book and carry it around with you just to show people you are a published author, you are doing more than enough to make major headway in establishing yourself as anexpert. But the key is you need at least one printed copy.

For most of you, you will get a lot more than one printed copy because once you write this book, you will be so proud of it that you will want to sell it on your website, on Amazon, and you will even enjoy giving free copies of it away to potential clients, employees, friends, and family. In fact, most of you will find that giving away a free copy of your book is one of the easiest ways of getting a meeting with that potential client you have wanted to meet for so long.

You see, when someone receives a book in the mail, along with a handwritten note from the author asking them to meet, it is very hard for them to say no. But why is it so hard for us to resist meeting the author of a book, even though I just finished telling you that any of you can have a book written and published in thirtydays? Up until very recently, it was incredibly difficult to write a book, because books had to be published through publishing houses. These big publishing houses had to invest significant amounts of money in every book, so it was very difficult to convince them to allow you to write a book. Recently, however, technology has allowed us to self-publish books with as few as one hundredbooks in a single run. Looking at authors as people who are above the rest of us is a centuries' old concept. We all have the impression that writing a book is actually much more difficult than it is in the current reality. Even though writing a book is as simple as talking into your phone for thirty minutes a day over a period of a month, when you have your book in hand, people will have a very different perception of what you have accomplished and who you are.

Put the excuses aside and start writing your book today, and enjoy being a published author in as little as thirty days from now – or more realistically, within six months.

Embrace social media marketing

Whether you do business-to-consumer (B2C) or business-to-business (B2B), you must embrace social media in order to take your business to the next level. Depending on your generation, you may or may not have already done this. Some individuals consider social media to be something that is just for play and do not take it seriously as a legitimate business tool. Others simply have not embraced social media yet, so they do not see the value that it can add to a business. A third group of folks, typically the younger generation, use social media as a place to have fun, but only embrace the platforms currently used by their peers.

Regardless of which of these three scenarios describes you, it is time that you embrace all of the most popular platforms for social media. Social media is here to stay and it is the future in terms of where business will be conducted. Social media is the place where you can teach people about your brand and inform individuals of what you do.

It used to be that branding was done with flyers, brochures, billboards, radio ads, and television commercials. But today, most people are spending more of their time on social media than in any other place. Additionally, social media gives us the opportunity to engage very targeted groups of people. For this reason, it is an absolute essential tool for marketing.

Besides, how many forms of marketing do you know of that are free? Imagine having the ability to access hundreds, thousands, and even millions of potential clients without paying a cent. That is what social media allows you to do, but you must be willing to embrace it and invest some time in building online communities. If you are not big on social media yourself and do not want to take the time to manage the accounts yourself, this is actually okay; you can hire people or companies to manage your accounts for you, but it is critical for you to establish and maintain a social media presence on most major platforms, including Facebook, Twitter, LinkedIn, Google +, Instagram, Pinterest, and believe it or not, even Myspace. This is certainly not an exhaustive list of social media outlets, but the basics that you must have in order to get started. Of course, not all platforms work for every business, so figure out which ones match your industry or your personality best, and focus on mastering them.

If you have not spent a lot of time promoting your business through social media channels, keep in mind that the key to social media is educational marketing. But you are now an expert at educational marketing, so all you are doing is essentially sharing the educational content that you're producing via social media. That is why this marketing system works so beautifully.

As long as you are focused on generating good educational content that adds value, you can share it across social media platforms and people will actually do your marketing for you by sharing what you have shared with them. If you have some extra time, you can also spend time engaging potential clients online by taking an interest in what they do by liking or commenting on things that they post. Make sure you are taking an interest in them and not just advertising your services. People do not like to be sold anything on social media. They are, though, more than happy to listen to what you have to say and learn from you. As long as you only put out a sales pitch every once in awhile, you will see the leads coming in like you've never seen before.

One great way of generating leads on social media without selling anyone anything is by creating some sort of a free giveaway, such as a free guide, and allowing people to download it in exchange for their information. This can be done very easily with a simple lead conversion page setup on your website where the user enters their name and email address, and the guide is emailed to them automatically. There are plenty of online tools, such as OptinMonster, for doing this that can be set up fairly easily without much assistance from experts. But if you need assistance from them, there are plenty of companies that can do this for you.

The key is that, in order to succeed in business today, you must embrace social media and have a substantial social media presence. This chapter is not intended to be a how-to on social media; it is simply intended to be the spark that motivates you to take action and become active in this particular outlet for your business. Once you have done that, you may want to consider expanding your knowledge by reading other books on the topic.

Now let's address the different groups of people mentioned earlier.

Those of who have yet to embrace social media:

If you have not embraced social media yet, please understand that social media is not going away. Unless you want to live in denial for the rest of your life, it's time you embrace it. You don't need to embrace it for yourself personally, but you do need to for your business.

Those who love social media but only like to play with it:

Social media is a great place to play and have a good time, but you must also use it for your business. If you are already a social media whiz, you have an advantage over others because you understand the landscape. Now you have to spend time doing social media with the intent of earning business, as opposed to just posting fun pictures of yourself.

Those who only use the coolest and newest channels – yes, I'm talking to you, Snapchatters - while the latest social media tool, such as Snapchat or whatever came out in the last few months, might be what all of the high school kids are using, it is important that you don't lose sight of where the core audience is hanging out. Tools like Twitter, Facebook, and LinkedIn are an absolute must. So if you are in the younger generation and you have not embraced these tools for yourself personally, that is okay. But you must embrace them for your business.

Chapter V

Without a Sales Funnel, You're Throwing Spaghetti at the Wall

Without a clearlydefined sales funnel and methods for tracking prospects as they flow through your sales funnel, you are probably missing out on over 50% of the business you could be converting, and over 90% of the prospects and leads you could be getting into your business. Unfortunately, most companies do not focus on an established sales funnel and most entrepreneurs do not think of having a tracked sales system, even though selling is by far the most important part of ensuring the success of your organization in the long term.

A sales funnel is simply a method of tracking what stage of the sale each potential client or prospect is in. In some businesses, for example, a sales funnel goes from Prospect to Lead to Qualified Lead to Negotiation and finally to Client.

Without a sales funnel, you are simply running around trying to make things happen. But once you have a sales funnel in place, the process of selling becomes very mathematical and simple to follow because things just lead from one step to the next.

FUNNEL

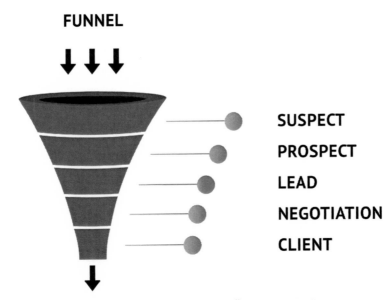

SUSPECT

PROSPECT

LEAD

NEGOTIATION

CLIENT

Salespeople fail because they just focus on "making sales"

After a quarter of a century in business and having been a salesperson myself for nearly a decade, it takes me only a few minutes to know if a salesperson is really as good as they claim to be. One of the simplest ways of analyzing who is truly a good salesperson and who is not is simply by listening to how they describe their sales activities. While this is a great tool for gauging if a salesperson is good at the job they are doingnow, it is unfortunately not as useful when hiring salespeople. Don't think of this so much as a hiring tool, but instead, look at these factors and see how you can become a much better salesperson as a result. Here are some of the mistakes that salespeople make:

1. **Laydown-based selling**. Unfortunately, many sales people fall into this category because it's the most convenient way of pretending like you are a salesperson without actually doing the hard work that all sales people are expected to do. The concept of "laydowns" come from my days as a sales counselor at Circuit City. In those days, I worked in the computer department and it was a very competitive atmosphere.

Some days, we would have to work hard to get people who were passing through the store to think about purchasing a computer. However, there were those lucky moments when a man or woman walked into the store at 4 p.m. on a Sunday and said,

"My daughter is going away to college tomorrow and I need a laptop for her." At that moment, we know we had a laydown and we were going to make an easy sale, with no work on our part.

2. **Handoff-based selling**. This type of salesperson is the one who is always telling you about the number of proposals they've sent out and how many sales they have almost ready to happen. It seems that most of their focus is on the lower portion of their sales funnel, but not actual sales, which are all the way at the bottom.

    These salespeople are the ones who seem to struggle the most, because their entire focus is on a few potential customers who they think they are going to be able to close. They do not talk much about their results in terms of conversions at the bottom of the funnel and they do not talk much about activity at the top of it, which traditionally involves prospecting, cold calling, and efforts to get more people into the sales funnel. These people start every day with the hope that the few leads they have stuck in the lower portion of the sales funnel will finally bite today.

    Every once in awhile, they reach out to these people and try to get them to move to the next stage, but it seems they are very satisfied with just the hope of these folks taking the plunge. As a result, they spend very little time looking for new prospects because they always believe they can close these few prospects. When you talk to these salespeople days, weeks, or, in some cases, even months later, they are often talking about the same leads and they almost always make you feel like they are on the brink of something truly amazing. But "truly amazing" rarely arrives, and when they do make a big sale, there is not much waiting on the horizon, other than big hopes and dreams for other sales stuck in the neck of the pipeline.

3. **Prayer-based selling**. Believe it or not, these people actually do better than the first group. This is the group that loves to make connections. Always out prospecting, they spend their time passing out business cards, brochures, flyers, and making connections every day. When you ask them how they are doing in terms of sales, they will tell you about the fact that they met thirty new people today at the Chamber of Commerce meeting or that they passed out fifty business cards at the last trade show. They will tell you that they recently met a C-level execu-

tive at one of the local corporations.

The problem with prayer-based salespeople is that rarely do you hear them talking about the activity in the middle and lower end of the funnel such as making presentations, having follow-up meetings, and,mostimportantly, making sales. This is because these individuals like to get to know people and enjoy making connections. They have the top of the sales funnel absolutely mastered, but they are typically not interested or are unable to sell or close the deal.

Unfortunately, these salespeople suffer significantly because they are not focused on over 75% of the sales funnel. However, they are able to make more sales than the first group simply because they have enough activity at the top of the sales funnel, regardless of their closing ratios and conversion rates from one step of the sales funnel to the next. For this reason, they will always have some people who need theproduct or service at a specific time and will consequently make a sale, but unfortunately, it is only on their terms and sales don't come anywhere near often enough.

4. **Results-based selling**. This is the group that typically makes up some of the best salespeople we know. When you ask these salespeople what they are doing, they always tell you about the number of sales they have or have not made. They never care to tell you about how many business cards they passed out and they could care less about the number of proposals they have made. Instead, when you ask them how they are doing in terms of sales, they either tell you how many sales they've made and tell you that they are having an incredible month, or they tell you the number of sales they've made and explain that they are very disappointed because their sales numbers are not where they should be.

    These people succeed because they do not live in a dream world, where the people to whom they pass out business cards will actually want to do business with them. They are not fooled by the few proposals they have out. Instead, when they have a proposal out, they will follow up with the individual consistently until they get the result they are after. They will either be told to go away or they will close the sale. But rarely do they let opportunities to make a sale sit in the funnel.

As you read this, you are probably starting to think that these salespeople are perfect and that they are the best. But it turns out there is one group that is even better than this group. That group typically does sales numbers that the other three groups can only dream of.

5. **Sales funnel-based selling**. This is truly the cream of the crop of salespeople. These are the salespeople who sell by the numbers. When you ask them how they are doing, they don't get bogged down with the details of any one thing. It's almost as if individual proposals, individual people they met, or individual sales they have recently made mean nothing to them. Those activities are simply numbers in their sales game.

When you ask these people what kind of a day, week, or month they are having, they will almost always tell you the details in numbers. They will use very few words but a lot of numbers to tell you how things are going. The most important factor about the numbers they tell you is that their numbers will be from all different parts of the sales funnel, including the top, the middle, and the bottom.

A car salesman who effectively uses a sales funnel will tell you, for example, that he spoke to twenty-five new leads today, including calling referrals, calling back former clients, and approaching several people on the lot. He will also tell you that he is excited about the fact that he did nine test drives today. Most of all, he was able to close two deals, one of which was on the clearance inventory that the dealership is currently making a big push for the salesmen to sell.

A real estate agent might tell you that he made one hundred cold calls, got fifteen people to actually listen to him without hanging up, made three appointments, and also had two appointments in the evening, of which he was able to get one of the listings.

Notice that these types of salespeople are all about the numbers. To them, it's a game. And while they may or may not know what a sales funnel is and they may or may not have it drawn out using fancy graphics, their mind thinks in terms of numbers – and not just numbers at the bottom or the top, but numbers in all of the different parts of the sales funnel.

Equipped with this knowledge, get out there and be the best sales-person you can possibly be for your company by establishing a sales funnel where you track prospects and leads all the way through, so you know at any point exactly how many people you have in each part of the sales funnel. Do this and you will see your sales dramatically increase.

The Five Levels of Salespeople... Which one are you?

- **Level 1**: Laydown-Based Sellers – Waiting for sales to come to them.
- **Level 2**: Handoff-Based Sellers – Sending proposals or making presentations and waiting for people to say yes.
- **Level 3**: Prayer-Based Sellers – Constantly trying to meet new people and make more connections in the hopes of getting clients.
- **Level 4**: Results-Based Sellers – Focused on making sales and tracking how much business they have done.
- **Level 5**: Funnel-Based Sellers – Focused on tracking every aspect of the sales process by the numbers including prospecting, qualifying leads, doing proposals, and closing sales.

The simplest way to increase business

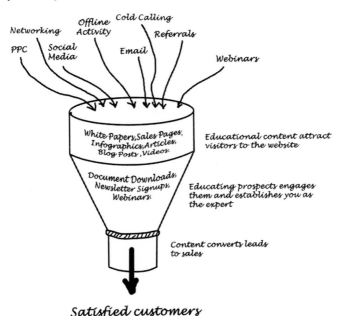

Regardless of what type of sales funnel you have, by far the easiest way to increase the number of sales you make is by increasing the number of prospects that go into the top of your sales funnel. I understand that I just finished telling you that the best salespeople are the ones who focus on every area of the sales funnel. But I also understand that most people are starting somewhere in one of those four areas. Regardless of which of those four categories you fall into, by far the best way to have an immediate impact on your sales is to increase the number of leads at the top of your sales funnel.

By far the easiest way of doing this, of course, is marketing. Since you are now an expert at educational marketing, you should have no problem getting massive numbers of prospects into the top of your sales funnel. But another way of getting prospects into the top of your sales funnel is making cold calls. I know some of you think of that as the worst thing in the world, but let me tell you that I have never met a great salesperson that does not make cold calls.

Focus on making cold calls, marketing, and getting as many people into the top of your sales funnel as possible, and watch your sales grow dramatically. The key is to focus on the numbers and track them, just as the best salespeople in the world do. Make sure that you are consistently tracking how many new prospects you get at the top of the sales funnel. This daily tracking will ensure that you stay on top of your sales funnel and will allow you to grow every part of your funnel, including the only part you get paid for: the bottom.

Optimize your sales funnel

Note: During this chapter, we will use the terms *suspect, prospect, lead, opportunity, potential customer,* and *potential client* interchangeably. In reality, most businesses will take each of these things to mean completely different things. Because of that, I want to use all of these terms, and for the purpose of this chapter, we will be using all of these terms interchangeably.

Let's assume you have the first two steps covered, meaning that you have a sales funnel set up where you are obsessed with the numbers – otherwise known as gamification – and you have focused on massively increasing the number of leads that go into the top of your funnel. If you have accomplished this and you are certain you are truly maximizing the number of leads that can go into the top of your sales funnel and you are honestly tracking all of the numbers within it and obsessing about them daily, weekly, and monthly, it is time to pour some serious fuel on this fire.

It is at this stage that we can start to gauge conversion rates. Conversion rates are essentially the rates at which leads move from one step of the sales funnel to the next. The key now is to analyze each step to the next. Let's assume you have a five-step sales funnel with the following labels:

1. **Suspects.** For you, suspects are those at the very top of your sales funnel. These could be people who have liked or commented on one of your social media posts, or leads in a list that you have purchased, or members of an organization to which you belong.

2. **Prospects.** Prospects are those who have gone one step further in this process. Potentially, these are the individuals with whom you have had some interaction. For example, you have exchanged business cards with them at a show or you have messaged with them back and forth on social media. Maybe you have cold called them and they have answered your phone call and not yet hung up on you.

3. **Leads.** These are the one you know are potentially qualified to be a customer for you. (Please note that this is just one example. These terms could mean very different things in a different sales funnel. For example, many companies might put *qualified prospect* at this stage. Additionally, for many organizations, the qualifying process happens before Step 2.)

4. **Presentation or Negotiation.** In this example, we are assuming that you have a sales cycle that includes some sort of a presentation or proposal that can be done either online, over the phone, or in person. But at this stage, the individual has completed the presentation stage.

5. **Sale.** This is the level at which you have now made a sale and attained the ultimate goal with this particular client.

Let's assume you are looking at activity from one single day, a week, or a month. Your conversion rates are going to be the percentage of each level that make it to the next level. For example, if you had 1,000 suspects to whom you made cold calls, and 100 of them picked up the phone and spoke to you without instantly hanging up, you can say your conversion rate from suspect to prospect is 10%. Now let's assume that of those 100 who have answered your phone call, 20 of them have some sort of an interest in your product or service, and you have qualified them to be potential prospects for you. This means that your conversion rate from prospect to lead is 20%. Now let's assume that you attempt to set up those 20 individuals for an in-person meeting. Some will say yes and others will say no. Additionally, of the ones who say yes, you will only be able to meet with some of them, because some will change their minds, schedules will get busy, and things will happen. But let's assume that five out of the 20 actually end up meeting with you for a presentation. That means that your conversion rate from lead to presentation given is 25%. Now, without any history, these numbers will not mean much. Once you have tracked these numbers for some time, however, you can start to see the trends in your particular business. This will allow you to figure out how to make minor changes that can make a big difference.

Make your sales explode

When you start to analyze the numbers, you realize why it is that I talk about the top of your sales funnel being by far the most important part to improve. Most businesses can easily double or triple the number of leads they have coming into the top of their sales funnel. But trying to double or triple the percentage of proposals they turn into sales is much, much more difficult. Consider this: if you are converting 40% of your sales by closing two out of every five proposals and you are able to double that, it would mean you are closing 80% of the proposals that you make.

The reality is that this is impossible to do. In most businesses, it would be almost impossible to go from closing 40% of your proposals to 80% of your proposals. However, doubling the number of suspects you get into the top of your sales funnel from 1,000 to 2,000 is very doable. This, by the way, is why you see the biggest companies in the world purchasing Super Bowl ads and spending millions of dollars on advertisements. By increasing the number of leads at the top of their sales funnel, they are making it significantly easier to make sales at the bottom of their sales funnel.

Of course, you cannot overlook the fact that no matter how many leads you get into the top of your sales funnel, you must have good closing ratios. But if you can make the small tweaks that improve your conversion rates, you are going to see sales skyrocket, regardless what is happening in every other part of your sales funnel. In order to get by far the best results, start with tracking the numbers. Once you are doing that, increase the number of leads into the top of your sales funnel. Once you have mastered that, analyze weaknesses within your conversion rates. Finally, make the small tweaks necessary in order to massively increase the number of sales you make.

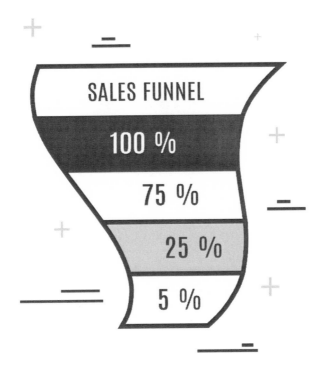

Chapter VI

Business Owner or Slave to Your Business?

For any business to grow and flourish, there must be documented operational systems. These documented systems not only allow you to achieve consistent results, but they also ensure that the results you produce are not dependent on the person who is doing the task. More importantly, things that you are able to make into systems can slowly be handed off to employees who will be able to do them every bit as well as you, and ideally, even better than you. The best companies in the world have mastered the art of creating systems and training their employees to follow them 100% so they can deliver the same results every time.

Of course, the best example of this is seen in franchise businesses, where their entire model is literally to create systems for operations that are so good that people would be willing to pay to tap into them. Your business may or may not be a franchise, but it is critical that you create operational systems that will allow you to maximize the quality that you provide while cutting costs and ensuring consistency.

PROCEDURE

1.

2.

3.

The chef who was a slave to his restaurant

I want to start by telling you the story of an Italian man who loved food and wine. He worked hard as a young kid, working in the back of kitchens washing dishes, and eventually working his way up the line until he finally becamea chef. His dream was realized when he finally opened his own Italian restaurant with his name on the outside of the building.

At this restaurant, which was his pride and joy, he served some of the most delicious Italian food anywhere in the United States. He had incredible recipes, outstanding customer service, great ambience, and restaurant reviews that catapulted him to the top of the most popular restaurant listing sites.

When he got married, he only took three days off for his honeymoon because the business needed him and he had to be there to make sure that things were on track. After all, he did all of the ordering, he was the one who made the special sauce, and it was him that the patrons wanted to see when they came to eat the restaurant. When his first son was born, he was at the hospital for a day and a half, but was constantly communicating with the people back at the restaurant to make sure things were going well.

Unfortunately, not everything went well because the birth came as a bit of a surprise – a few months sooner than expected – and he was not prepared, so he received his first one-star review on Yelp as a result. When his second son was born, again by surprise, he was a bit more prepared. But this time, due to some complications, he had to be out of the restaurant for most of one week. During this time, customer service fell to an all-time low. He received some negative reviews; unfortunately, one of those was from a critic who happened to visit the restaurant during the time he was gone.

Some of his most loyal customers said that they were excited for him to get back because they wanted to eat at his restaurant again, but others simply moved on. During that week, the quality of his food suffered, customer service suffered, and even employee morale suffered, because he was always the one holding everything together.

Eventually, after two decades of working hard to keep his restaurant afloatand doing everything he could, he got older and was not able to spend as much time as the restaurant needed. Gradually, business slowed down, and when the economy fell, he was forced to shut down the restaurant. Looking back, he realized that he didn't have an incredible restaurant; he was an incredible employee. He provided the best customer service. He made sure that everything was ordered on time and in the right amounts. He made sure to cut costs wherever he could. He prepared the most important parts of the food, and he provided the recipes. The problem was he did absolutely everything.

As I write this book, my number one goal is to help you establish an organization that will be much bigger than just you. I want you to have a company thatthrives, not a business to which you are a constant slave. I want you to be a business owner, not a day-to-day operator of your business. Now don't get me wrong; if you enjoy what you do, there is nothing wrong with you operating the business, being an employee of it, and even working seven days a week, 365 days a year. But when the time comes, if you choose to take a day, a week, a month, or even a year off, your business should be set up in a way that it allows you to do so without suffering substantially.

Without systems, you will always be a slave to your business

The key to freeing yourself frombeing a slave to your business is to develop operational systems that allow you and your employees to get results on a consistent basis, using a proven set of steps that get the same result every single time. The classic example everyone mentions is McDonald's. Here is a restaurant with thousands of locations across the entire world that serves essentially the same menu and produces almost the same thing every time. You can order a Big Mac in California, New York, Paris, Athens, or Beijing and get essentially the same thing every time. That is the power of documented operational systems.

When you walk into a Subway sandwich shop, not only do you get the same results, but everything is laid out in front of you exactly the same way in every single restaurant. The order in which various ingredients are placed into a sandwich is the same every time. For example, if you order a turkey sandwich, they always select the bread first, place the meat inside of the bread, followed by cheese and a certain set of vegetables that are part of the first step, and then a second set of vegetables that are a part of the second step. Finally, they ask you if you would like oil and vinegar, followed by salt and pepper.

This massively oversimplifies their process, but the key is that no matter what city or country in the world you are in, lettuce always comes before bell peppers, meat always comes before cheese, and salt and pepper always come last. In some cases, these things make sense. For example, placing the meat first, followed by the cheese makes sense, especially if you are going to have the sandwich toasted. But in other cases, there is no apparent reason for certain vegetables to be put in before others. However, the systems are still in place because creating the same result every time using a proven set of systems is how you can stop being a slave to your business. By doing things the same way every time, you don't have to spend time thinking about how to do them. You just do.

If you are not able to create systems because there are things you do that only you know how to do, while you may get good results, you will always be a slave to your business and it will always require you in order to get those same results. The key is to document the things that you do, how you do them, and why you do them, in exactly the order in which you do them. Eventually, you can have your business work for you as opposed to you constantly working for your business.

But even if you do have the business working for you, and you have employees who are doing the work and doing a great job at it, it is still important to have them working off of documented operational systems. Employees can decide to leave you or could have issues beyond their control which will cause them to not be able to perform at their best. Do not be a slave to your business by failing to create documented operational systems.

People-dependent businesses always fail in the end

One of the keys to having a successful business is having a systems-dependent business with very good people working inside of those systems, as opposed to a people-dependent business. No matter how good your employees are and no matter how great the culture you build within your organization, if you build a people-dependent company, in the end, it will always fail.

The problem with a dependence on people is that people go through various stages of their lives. They unfortunately have accidents, they have bad days and good days, they have bad years and good years. They may also decide to leave you to go work for someone else or even leave you because they want to start a competing business or one in a completely different sector.

There are many small companies that do extremely well because the business owner is very good at hiring the best people and keeping them motivated. While this approach works extremely well in some cases, it is a dangerous road to go down. If your business succeeds because it has very good people who make good decisions, are well trained, and follow directions well, you are always at the mercy of those people. No matter how good they are or how good you are at finding them, you will eventually find that your people-dependent company will slowly or quickly come tumbling down.

This is not to say that people are not important. In fact, I can tell you that your employees are by far the most important assets you have in any organization. However, the key is to understand that instead of hiring great employees first, your focus should be on building great operational systems first and then hiring great people to work within those systems. It is simply a matter of the order in which you do things.

By starting with your operations first, you will not only establish a solid system to make sure you are not people-dependent, but you will also ensure that the best employees are able to perform at an even higher level. This is because they don't have to spend time thinking about what to do, they can just do it, leaving time to innovate within the job and improve your company.

You see, when you give someone a set of guidelines to follow that are clearly written out and strict, they don't have to spend their mental energy trying to figure out what to do next. Instead, they follow the systems and then innovate. And if your best employee decides to leave you, has a baby, or is out for two weeks, your business does not suffer anywhere near as much, because it is much easier to hire someone to come in and follow the same system that your employee followed.

Document all procedures

There are many ways of documenting procedures for how things should be done. The simplest is to just use Microsoft Word or Google Docs to begin documenting your procedures in a simple outline. If you open up a Google Doc, or a Word document, at the top of the page, you can put the name of the procedure, such as "How to Make a Web Presentation for Our XYZ Services."

Underneath it, you can put a quick sentence that lays out some details about this procedure. For example, you could say, "When you have an online presentation scheduled for a potential client, follow this procedure so you can be sure to do everything correctly from A to Z." Then you click the little number button at the top of Word or Google Docs that will start your outline and you can start listing the steps, as seen below.

> Step 1: Schedule the meeting using GoToMeeting
> Step 2: Send reminder email to client
> Step 3: Start presentation with GoToMeeting five minutes before the scheduled start time

Now that you have a basic outline, you can tab down beneath each step and write some of the details for each particular step. In fact, you could include a link to GoToMeeting or you could include some different items that might be necessary for this step.

From here, you can go on to have a link to the actual PowerPoint presentation that might be used. You can even include various scripts and different things that are needed for the process. The point is that if you weren't there, someone else could take your step-by-step standard operating procedure (SOP) and follow it in order to get similar results.

Now of course, not everything can be put into an SOP. Just because you have an SOP does not mean someone is going to get exactly the same results that you would. But I think you would agree it is a much better place to start than with a blank piece of paper. Additionally, when you have an SOP, you can now have people observe you while you make a presentation and you can train them by having them follow along with you as they listen and watch.

What you will notice is that they are going to retain much more of the information than they would if they were just listening. Some of the simple things you do such as setting up the meeting five minutes before the start time might be overlooked, or certain things that you say that are important to your script may be completely missed if someone just listens to you. But if these things are documented, they know that they are not happening on accident and are in fact a part of the way you do the system.

This is why when you walk into many restaurant chains, including some of the newer ones that have recently launched, they have policies on exactly what kind of a greeting you are going to receive. For example, the ice cream chain Creamistry has a policy where every employee on the floor will greet every person who walks in. So every time the door opens and people come in, everyone says, "Hi, how are you doing?" or "Hi! Hello!"

The point is that they don't want the employees to make a decision as to whom they will and will not greet. While this may seem like a minor point, when you look at businesses that are operated by the owner, this is something a business owner almost always naturally does. But once you hire a group of seventeen-year-old kids to work at your restaurant, they may not have the same level of experience and will not see the importance of saying hello to everyone who walks in.

One of the tools I have used for standard operating procedures is an online tool called Sweet Process, found at sweetprocess.com. This is a way of having a centralized location for all of your procedures that can be accessed from anywhere on the internet by anyone with a link. The application is also built to be mobile-friendly, so you can easily bring up procedures on a cell phone. We have even embedded some of these procedures into our website and share them with clients at my digital marketing company, so clients can follow procedures that we have created for them.

While it does not do a lot that Microsoft Word or Google Docs cannot do, it is a very good way of centralizing everything and keeping your standard operating procedures organized. Either way, focus on building standard operating procedures for your business and having them documented, because it is these procedures that are going to allow you to thrive in the future and ensure that you will never be a slave to your business. More importantly, with high-quality SOPs in place, you will never be a slave to a people-dependent company, whether the people are your employees or you yourself.

Why the Subway model works

As we discussed earlier, the sandwich chain Subway is one of the best examples of great operational systems created in order to franchise a business. First of all, let's recognize that Subway has been one of the fastest growing franchises on the planet over the past two decades. They have managed to grow much faster than the competition and have expanded into just about every market in the United States as well assome of the biggest markets in the world.

There are many things that Subway does well, but what it does better than anything else is having very simple and clearly defined operations procedures. By documenting every step of the procedure and taking the guesswork out, Subway has managed to build a brand that has allowed entrepreneurs all over the world to start their own businesses and make a good living operating their stores. Of course, at the same time, Subway the corporation has done extremely well and raked in some huge profits as a result.

To see the true value of operations systems, let's consider why some-one would open a Subway franchise, instead of just opening their own sandwich shop. It would seem that you could take all the best practices that Subway has in place and then even add your own on top of it and have a better system. But the reality is it is not easy to do that. When you own a franchise for Subway, there is a very specific way that everything is done. Not only are sandwiches made according to very specific recipes and employees trained in very specific ways, but their model goes far beyond this.

The way that tomatoes are cut in the back are done according to a standard operating procedure, for example. While this may not seem like a big deal, it is an essential part to the system that Subway has created, because inefficiencies are eliminated by having vegetables chopped in a specific manner at a specific time of the day in a specific place. This allows franchise operators to ensure that they are not dealing with the things that typical restaurants do.

In a typical restaurant, the thickness of the tomatoes is going to be different depending on who is cutting them and what kind of a mood they're in. Additionally, typical restaurants often run out of various ingredients throughout the day. While it is easy to chop up some additional tomatoes, it is not an efficient way of running a business by any stretch of the imagination. Additionally, when people are left to decide when, how, and where to chop tomatoes and other vegetables, they have a tendency of spending more of their time thinking about the action, rather than just doing it.

By having a documented procedure in place, it gets employees to immediately take action and it gives the franchise operator an easy way of tracking if people are doing their jobs. It is very simple to look around and see if all of the vegetables have been chopped by a specific time in the morning before opening. If they have not been chopped, it will be easy to see and appropriate action can be taken.

So take notice the next time you go into a Subway of just how much of the business is following a very specific protocol, as opposed to relying on chance or on good employees. Of course, the operator of a Subway franchise still works hard to hire the best employees he or she can hire. But they certainly do not need to try to find the best of the best employees and pay an extremely high salary just to have a good quality food and service. They certainly do not need to hire a chef, and they themselves do not need to be one or even know how to make a sandwich, because the operations manual gives them all of that information.

Take the time today to go into a Subway sandwich shop. From the minute you enter the restaurant, look at how scientific everything is, from the layout of the restaurant to the tables and chairs, the decorations on the walls, the uniforms the employees wear, the way the food is laid out, the way your order is taken, and the way you proceed through the line. If you want to see a true test of just how amazing Subway's systems are, go to a busy Subway location at about 12:15 in the afternoon and watch just how efficiently this restaurant gets things done at the busiest time of the day.

A procedure for your procedures?

Regardless of what system you choose to use for tracking your policies and procedures, the key is to keep all of your procedures centralized and to have an effective way of tracking which procedures are in fact live and which are in draft mode. This can be accomplished by using several possible methods, including a Word document, Google Docs, an Excel spreadsheet, Google Sheets, or a program such as Sweet Process.

It is critical that systems that are live be used every single time, since creating a culture where systems are used when needed but not necessarily enforced every single time can be very dangerous. The whole point of a system is that it happens the same way every single time. Keep track of your live procedures and policies in a single place and check them on a regular basis to ensure that they are up to date and being enforced.

If something cannot be enforced, I highly recommend that you remove the procedure from your master list until the day that it can be enforced. You are better off having a procedure manual with five procedures that are followed than having one thousand procedures that are not actually being followed. Focus on centralizing your systems into one place and use the many different tools I have outlined in this chapter. You will have a level of freedom most business owners can only dream of achieving. If you take the lessons in this chapter to heart, I want to congratulate you on the fact that you will officially be a business owner and not a business operator, a feat most business owners never accomplish in their lifetime.

<u>Chapter VII</u>

Create "Raving Fan"
Customers & Employees

As a company committed to growth, you must be committed to consistently creating "raving fan" customers and "raving fan" employees. The term "raving fan", coined by Ken Blanchard and Sheldon Bowles in their book *Raving Fans*, means that while everyone else is struggling to keep their employees happy and to make sure the needs of their customers are met, your goal is to step up to a level that is much higher than anything they could ever dream of. Your goal is to turn every relationship with employees and clients into a raving fan relationship. That means going above and beyond for employees and for every customer in every transaction in order to consistently create raving fans that will truly rave about your product or service on a consistent basis.

Satisfied customers are useless

Have you ever considered the value of a "satisfied customer?" What does having a satisfied customer truly add to the bottom line of your business? Let's take a moment to consider the behavior of a satisfied customer. First of all, let's consider that in order to have a customer or client vendor relationship, there is basically going to be some sort of an exchange of products or services for money.

A satisfied customer is one who is paying for some sort of a product or service, receiving that product or service, and then making a determination that he or she feels satisfied about the transaction. That means, by definition, he or she feels the amount of money paid is relatively the same as the services rendered. Therefore, it means that the individual's expectations have been met.

But do people rave to others about their expectations being met? Do people remember vendors that provided them services where their expectations were met? Do people go out of their way to do business with vendors who have simply met their expectations and their needs? The answer for the most part is no.

If we pay $3 for dry cleaning at ABC Dry Cleaners and we feel that the service we received was worth about $3, we are not going to drive halfway across town to go back to that dry cleaners because, psychologically, we assume that every drycleaner would give us $3 worth of dry cleaning in exchange for that same amount. In order to get us to drive across town, we have to feel like we received a lot more than what we paid for. At the same time, we would not go to the office that day and randomly tell one of our colleagues about the "satisfied experience" we had at ABC Dry Cleaners. There is nothing to rave about, nothing to get excited about, and nothing to talk about, other than the fact that we expected $3 worth of services, so we paid $3 and we received what we expected.

If weeks or months later we are randomly looking for a drycleaner, it is doubtful that our dealings with ABC Dry Cleaners was memorable enough that we would remember them and know exactly where they are located, what their website is, or what their phone number is so that we can immediately do business with them. Instead, we might go right back to searching, such as doing a Google search, looking on Yelp, or asking friends.

For these reasons, satisfied customers are completely useless when it comes to a business. In order to truly grow and expand your business, you must learn how to create raving fans!

Satisfied employees aren't good enough

Is your goal to have satisfied employees within your company? If it is, I want you know that you will find it almost impossible to create long-lasting relationships with employees who will want to do whatever it takes to help grow your company. While it is bad to have dissatisfied employees, believe it or not, it is almost as bad—and in some cases, worse—to have nothing but satisfied employees.

When you have dissatisfied employees, they are often very vocal with you, with management, and even on various online review sites. It is easy to find out what you are doing wrong and make adjustments, if you so desire. Additionally, dissatisfied employees can actually help make your company better by giving you the opportunity to turn them from dissatisfied employees to extremely happy employees, because you can create an environment for them that will allow them to thrive.

But even if you do not create that environment, dissatisfied employees typically will be very active in finding another job, so they will leave your company or they will underperform and you will eliminate them from your company, thereby getting them out of your organization. Often, the most valuable employees who are dissatisfied will not just go find another job or say negative things about your company behind closed doors. Instead, they will typically come to you and express their dissatisfaction so changes can be made.

Let's contrast that with satisfied employees. When you have a culture of satisfied employees, negative information does not really make its way back to you, because the employees for the most part are satisfied and do not have much to complain about. The problem with this is that it means the lowest performers in your company will not actively seek out other positions because they are typically happy gliding along. But the best employees in your company who are top performers will consistently be sought after by others.

Therefore, even though they are not looking for an opportunity to move to another company, great opportunities will naturally find them. And as opportunities come up, even though they are completely satisfied with working with your company, when an opportunity arises that allows them to go to the next level, they will often take that opportunity and grow. Before or after they leave your company, they will not complain about horrible conditions and they will not come to you with suggestions on how to make the company even better, because they really don't have complaints. They just don't have a compelling enough reason to immediately shut down anyone who suggests that they consider changing career paths. In the long run, with a culture that brews satisfied employees, you will end up creating an environment of mediocrity, and while thisis head and shoulders above a culture of dissatisfied employees, it is nothing like a culture filled with raving fan employees who love their jobs, love what you stand for, and will do whatever it takes to take the company to the next level.

Create a culture of raving fans about your brand

Now we can all see that satisfied customers and satisfied employees are completely useless, so the goal is to replace them with raving fans. Moreover, let's not just create one or two raving fans; your goal is to create a raving fan culture amongst your clients. While this is done differently in different industries and for different types of products and services, it can be accomplished in essentially any industry.

The way you know you have a raving fan culture amongst your clients is that they are responsible for selling more of your products and services than all of your salespeople and you marketing efforts combined. I drive a Tesla and I have told at least two hundredother people that they should get a Tesla – even random people I meet by chance – because I am without a doubt a raving fan of the auto company. Prior to my Tesla, I owned Mercedes cars for fifteen years. While I loved all of my cars, I don't believe I was responsible for a single sale of one of their cars. The reason is not that I was unsatisfied with my car or that I was unsatisfied with the services they provided me. In fact, I feel that all of my Mercedes cars were incredible and I have received nothing but the best services from Mercedes. I can tell you that I have always been a truly satisfied customer of the Mercedes brand and have absolutely nothing bad to say about them.

The key, however, is that with Mercedes, I feel that I got what I paid for. However, with Tesla, I feel that I would be willing to pay twice as much for what I have today. I feel that I am so far beyond a satisfied customer that nothing Tesla could do would make me say negative things about them. Interestingly enough, I have had two negative experiences with Tesla, but I have never had a negative experience with Mercedes. So how can it be that I am a raving fan of Tesla and just a satisfied customer for Mercedes?

The reason is simple. I am such a raving fan of the brand, my car, and the things it gives me that I am very willing to forgive them for their shortcomings. The car has so many amazing features; it just does so much and it is so far ahead of the rest of the industry that there is nothing else like it.In fact, I would never blame Tesla for the poor customer service I experienced on those occasions. Instead, I blame the individual person, which may not seem like a big distinction, but it is. Raving fans will forgive you for negative experiences by thinking to themselves that it was simply your employee who made a mistake, that you were having a bad day, or that the issue is an anomaly. But satisfied customers will quickly turn into dissatisfied customers as soon as issues arise.

In the same manner, I am a raving fan of Apple and other brands that I believe in wholeheartedly. While creating this raving fan culture is obviously an incredibly powerful idea, it is not as easy to create as one might think. It involves every aspect of your business and every person who has a hand in dealing with your customers. To create a raving fan culture, you cannot cut corners with customer service, product development, providing your services, or anything else you do, because your clients will not rave about your products and services fanatically if you do not go over the top every single time.

But creating a raving fan culture goes even beyond providing exceptional products and services. It also needs social proof. What that means is, as you start developing raving fans or extremely satisfied clients at first, you must showcase their experience and put it out for other satisfied clients to see. In this way, clients who are very satisfied might decide to join the group of raving fans and you will have raving fans causing other raving fans. Eventually, something beautiful and magnificent happens, and that is where 50% or more of your business will come from referrals from raving fans. The beauty of this is those who are referred by a raving fan essentially start out as being raving fans already. All you have to make sure is that you don't mess that up.

Therefore, you will reach a critical mass at one point where your raving fans will give you other automatic raving fans, especially because those raving fanatically about your products and services will help you attract others who are very much like them. Therefore, the demographics of your clients, whether businesses or consumers, will give you the ability to provide an even higher level of service. Whatever you do, focus on creating raving fans within your company on a consistent basis and develop that raving fan mentality and culture for your brand.

Once you have raving fan clients, you can tap into their excitement about your business by asking them to share their experience with the world. There are four levels, starting with the most basic to the most valuable:

Level 1: Ask your raving fan client if it would be okay for you to share their positive experience and story via your website and social media.

Level 2: Ask your raving fan client to provide you with a testimonial that you can include and quote them on your website as well as social media.

Level 3: Ask your raving fan client to make a social media post themselves talking about the wonderful experience they have had. This not only adds credibility but it also allows you to have exposure to their audience.

Level 4: Ask your raving fan client to make a quick video where they talk about their experience with you and why they are such a raving fan. This adds yet another layer, because you get everything from above but this also allows others to identify with them and connect with them, which will go a long way in getting you new clients.

Raving fan employees create raving fan customers

One of the easiest ways of starting the wave to having raving fan customers is to start by ensuring a culture of raving fan employees internally. This is not to say that every one of your employees raves about the job that they do on a daily basis. In fact, in many companies such as Apple, people have historically complained somewhat about the expectations of the job. But at the same time, they are raving fans of the products and services that the company offers.

In the same manner, your goal is to create a culture where you are doing more to market your products and services to your employees than you are even to your customers. It means "selling" what you do to your employees first and your customers second. Of course, you can hit a grand slam if you are able to create a culture where your employees not only believe in your products and services wholeheartedly, but they also love what they do and love the team they are a part of. Most importantly, they love what the company stands for and they are behind it 100%.

There are many amazing books written about creating an incredible culture within your organization, and I would recommend investing in educating yourself on the various ways in which you can create an incredible culture within your company. Once you have created raving fans within your organization, you will find that these raving fan employees will consistently develop raving fan customers, because they will go above and beyond in order to provide exceptional and outstanding customer service.

It is your employees, not you, who are typically interacting with the customer. Therefore, ensuring that you keep them 100% happy and sold on what your company stands for will ensure that they provide over-the-top customer service for your customers. Keep in mind that most employees treat your customers the way you treat them as employees. If you do not treat them well, they will not treat your customers well. On the other hand, if you treat them well and give them plenty of opportunities for growth, they will return the favor by providing similarly high quality customer service to your customers, thereby helping you create raving fan customers.

Raving fan employees make sales no matter what their title

Wouldn't it be nice to instantaneously grow your sales team without actually having to hire any new salespeople? Of course, we would all love that. Believe it or not, this may not be as hard as you think. Employees who are raving fans of the company, regardless of what their role may be, will always be out there selling for your company, and they can in fact do better at selling your products and services than salespeople who have been through years and years of sales training but are not raving fans themselves.

The reason is simple: selling is almost always a process of enthusiastically selling to someone how something is going to solve a problem for them and address some of their pain points. Raving fan employees do this naturally, because when they hear someone has a pain point that your product or service can resolve, they will be so ecstatic about what your company can offer that they will not be able to hold themselves back. As a result, prospective clients will be drawn in.

It doesn't matter if their role in the company is inhuman resources, operations, or even working in the warehouse. If they are raving fans of your company, they will get to know your products and services and they will take any opportunity they can to talk about your products and services to people. This will also assist in helping you sell more of your products and services to current customers, because individuals who are interfacing with them on a daily basis will consistently be excited about sharing new things with them and telling them what more your company can offer.

Focus on creating a culture of raving fans, inside and outside of your company. Raving fans are going to make your job much easier, and even more importantly, they are going to make your job more enjoyable. To get to this point, though, you must focus on having a clear goal of developing a raving fan culture.

Chapter VIII

Create Peace of Mind with a KPI Dashboard

The single most important tool for any business owner or CEO to be able to manage his or her company is a key performance indicator (KPI) dashboard. A KPI dashboard is simply a place you can visit that gives you a visual representation of how your company is doing with a set of numbers and gauges. The best dashboards in the world are so easy to read that within ten seconds of reading it, you know 80% of the information you need to run your company. If you keep looking and dig a bit deeper, you should know 95% of the most important things about what is going on within a company after just sixty seconds. This means the information shown on your KPI dashboard must be summarized and limited to only the most critical things in your business. Without a KPI dashboard, you as a CEO are driving a car without being able to see out of the windshield. Of course, it would be impossible to drive a car if your windshield was completely covered, yet so many business owners run their companies that way.

KPI STATUS

SALES

% MARKET

BUDGET

PEOPLE

Run your business from a remote island

There is a scenario I have created which I have been sharing with entrepreneurs and CEOs for over a decade, and it has helped many of my business coaching clients take their businesses to new heights. It is a simple concept that any of you could implement within your business with some focus and dedication. The takeaway lesson from this concept is that you must build a vast array of systems within your company to make it possible to run your business from a remote island. If you set this as a goal for your company, you will be able to achieve some incredible things as a result, even if you don't ever make it your reality.

The concept revolves around you creating a KPI dashboard that is so precise and well created that if you were on a remote island with no more than sixty seconds of internet access, split into two thirty-second increments, you could run your entire business working no more than ten minutes per day. In this scenario, let's assume that on your island you have thirtyseconds of internet access every morning at 8:00 a.m., followed by nine minutes of no internet, then thirty more seconds of internet access, followed by 23 hours and 50 minutes without any access whatsoever.

The goal in this scenario is to be able to effectively run your entire business working only from 8:00 a.m. to 8:10 a.m., and with internet access for only those two thirty-second slots. Let's consider what you would have to have in place in order to make this a reality. Immediately you recognize that you would have to have already eliminated your position as a day-to-day operator within your business. That means you would have had to build operational systems using SOPs and processes that allow your team to get high quality results without your constant presence.

Additionally, you would have to have systems, whether manual or automated, that capture the most critical aspects of your business in a simple KPI dashboard, so that the data can be transmitted to you in under thirty seconds every morning at 8:00 a.m. Then the data has to be so easy to understand that you should be able to look at it, understand it, and make critical business decisions based on that data in just a few minutes. In fact, within nine minutes, the goal is for you to make decisions about all of the tweaks, adjustments, and changes that need to be made and create key communication that can then be transmitted to your team at 8:09 a.m. during the second thirty-seconds of availability.

Of course, the purpose of playing this little game is to see if you could actually run your business in this manner. I don't necessarily want you to go to an island and run your business in this manner (although that is what some of you may decide to do after you implement the systems outlined in this book). The concept here that I want you to understand is that if you have a proper KPI dashboard and proper systems for communications in place within your company, then with the simple transmission of some basic data, you should be able to see where your company is, how it is doing, and where adjustments may need to be made.

In most cases when you see the numbers, you will find that adjustments are not necessary and that the things you already have in place are moving you in the right direction. At the same time, you may find that some adjustments must be made on specific days, weeks, and months. In those situations, you will make the appropriate adjustments with simple communication back to your team.

While this may seem like a far-fetched idea, imagine how the world's jumbo jets fly around the planet for hours and hours with no more than this type of information. In fact, spaceships are sent into space, around the moon, and even all the way to Mars using very similar concepts. The key of course is that you must have very, very good metrics, which means you must look at the most important things and you must know what those numbers mean within your operations. If they are not headed in the right direction, you need to know how to change course.

A byproduct of all of this, of course, is that once you have this KPI system in place, you can take time off from your business. Although you may not be on an island with only thirty seconds or one minute of internet access, you will now be able to travel with your family and have fun with your friends without being constantly connected to your electronic devices. In just a few minutes a day, you will be able to see how the business is doing and react accordingly.

What would driving be like without a gas gauge?

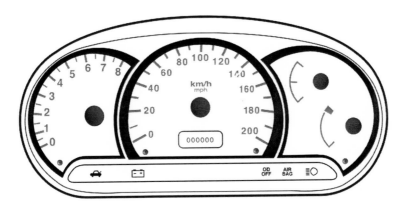

Now that you understand what a KPI dashboard is and what it's used for, let's start to talk about what a KPI dashboard might look like. Believe it or not, we are all very familiar with KPI dashboards. In fact, just about every single person reading this book has used a KPI dashboard almost every single day of his or her lives. Most of us would be completely lost without some of the critical KPI dashboards that we use on a regular basis.

The best example of a KPI dashboard that we all use on almost a daily basis is the one in our car. As you drive in your car, you have in front of you a speedometer that tells you how fast you're traveling, an RMP gauge that tells you how your engine is doing, a fuel gauge tells you how much gas you have, a temperature gauge that indicates the temperature of your car, and you might even have a navigation system that tells you where you are on a map. Additionally, you have controls that indicate what gear the engine is operating, and if you drive an electric vehicle, there's something that displays your power consumption and how much you have remaining, along with a variety of key performance indicators that tell you how your car is doing overall.

The beauty of this KPI dashboard is it's designed in an efficientway that allows you to do what you normally do without having to constantly watch all of the metrics on your KPI dashboard. This is exactly how your business should be run. It is not important to know every single metric within your companyon a daily basis. In fact, it would be quite a nuisance to have to look at all of those numbers on a daily basis. In your car, for example, looking at the temperature ten to fifteentimes during your commute would be a terrible waste of your time and would possibly distract you from more important things, such as your speed or what is happening on the other side of your windshield.

That's why the KPI dashboard in your car has some features that make it much more practical. For example, you are not bothered by your temperature gauge unless the temperature of your car rises to an abnormal level. In this case, the car warns you with a variety of lights and/or sounds. Your fuel gauge is much the same and has various levels, including a light that turns on when you are running low on fuel.

Certain gauges have a safe zone, typically marked by green, and other zones that are either too high or too low as indicators that something may not be in a nominal range. While your dashboard will track a variety of things, it is not important for all of those numbers to be in front of you on a daily basis. The KPI dashboard of your company should work in exactly the same way.

Many of the numbers tracked on your KPI dashboard should only warn you and raise a red flag when they reach certain levels. Yet for other key performance indicators, it is critical that you look at them on a daily basis and understand how your business is impacted by them. So as you begin to plan out your company's KPI dashboard, think of the one in your car and use the same concepts for your own.

What do you track and how often?

As you attempt to figure out the most important indicators within your organization to track, start with the numbers that you already look at on a regular basis that tell you quite a lot about your business. For example, most people are already looking at financial statements and looking at total revenue, net profit, and other things like that (I'll address specifics in a later chapter). If there are numbers you are already looking at on a regular basis, it's very good to start there with things that you are currently able to easily track, instead of trying to find numbers that are complex. Next, think of some of the numbers from your sales funnel that we have already discussed, such as the number of prospects, leads, cold calls, and ratios of things, such as percentage of leads converted into sales.

Next, you can think of things related to human resources, such as the number of employees, the cost of payroll, and things like that. Many companies already track things such as customer satisfaction scores, which can be gauged based on a survey that you conduct, or if you are in a business where clients regularly rate your business through online services such as Yelp, you can simply track your online rating.

But as you look at these numbers, regardless of what you've chosen, make sure you pay just as close attention to how often you are tracking things as what you track. Tracking things too often or not often enough can lead to a KPI dashboard that is too cumbersome or difficult to assess. For example, it may seem very possible to track customer service scores on a daily basis. But for most businesses, these are not numbers that are easily tracked on a daily basis and they often are not fluid enough to change a lot from day-to-day. There's no need to track them on a daily basis. Instead, this is a metric you may track on a monthly basis. Additionally, much of the things that relate to a company's finances may be numbers that you can only track on a monthly basis.

On the other hand, things that are very fluid and easy to capture, such as traffic to a website, the number of cold calls, and sales, may be things that you will want to track every day. Simply make a list of all the key performance indicators that are going to allow you to track where your company is. Remember as you are doing this, the most important thing is that your KPIs give youenough information for you to run your entire company from an island with only tenminutes of access. Therefore, they must paint a complete picture for you.

If you typically walk around the office, looking to see who is working and who might be browsing the internet, you certainly will not be able to do that from an island. You will need to consider ways of tracking things like that on a KPI dashboard. Or you may need to track metrics that are affected when individuals are less than perfectly efficient at work. The ultimate goal is to have numbers and metrics representing every aspect of your business so you are not having to guess what is going on within your company. Instead, you are able to focus on doing what you do best.

Finally, some of the best KPI dashboards in the world are those that have individual metrics that then lead to other metrics. You do not look at every metric every time; instead, if certain metrics are not where you would expect them to be, then you have the option of moving to more detailed metrics that break the bigger metrics into various compartments. That is what leads us to the ultimate purpose of KPIs and how they should be used.

Would you want a treasure map without "X" marking the spot?

The final concept to consider and learn before you implement your KPI dashboard is to understandthat it is not designed to be a how-to guide. Instead, it is designed to be more like a treasure map. What is the difference between a treasure map and a how-to guide? Well, the how-to guide provides all of the details you need about how to get a specific result, where to find things, and what to do when you get there. A treasure map is typically a single sheet of paper that you can look at quickly, and there is almost always an X somewhere on the map, marking the spot where the treasure is supposed to be. Your goal is to use the treasure map to simply dig around the area where there's an X.

A treasure map does not tell you how to dig, how deep to dig, and other details about what treasure you will find when you dig there. Additionally, it does not tell you the exact path to get there. All it provides you is some basic feedback on where you should take a deeper look. In fact, most treasure maps are wrong and will send you to go dig in places where you will not find any useful treasures.

KPI dashboards work very much in the same way. Most of the time, the information provided by a KPI dashboard will simply guide you in a particular direction and suggest you look further into something. This is what I call "dig here." Often, a KPI dashboard will point something out that appears to be of concern. But when you get there and dig further, you find that the anomaly is nothing outside of the ordinary and that there is nothing you want to do about it, which is perfectly fine. But the key is that it tells you where to look.

An example of this might be that on December 24thfor your B2B business, your KPI for the number of suspects looking at your website (unique website visitors) might be down a staggering 60% over your thirty-day running average. But this is perfectly acceptable for a B2B business because most companies are closed on Christmas Eve, and you will not be getting as much traffic. Therefore, your KPI dashboard will show something that would initially concern you, but then once you quickly dig and realize that this is simply an anomaly that is perfectly explained by the day of the month, you will move on with your day.

The key is that your KPI dashboard will always provide you with the information and tell you when you've reached an alarming level for anything. Once you confirm where you are, you will dig deeper and find out what there is to discover there. The best KPI dashboards in the world are those that, at just a glance, allow you to decide what is going on. Although I said in my desert island example that you have two minutes of total internet connection and eight minutes to analyze the data, in reality, it should take you no more than one minute to see what is going on. The rest of the time would be spent coming up with a game plan on how you are going to address the issue or spent digging deeper into the issue.

You can download a free guide to help you put your KPI dashboard together by visiting: titaniumsuccess.com/business-toolkit.

Chapter IX

Ultimate Financial Analysis Cheat Sheet (Don't let your CPA see this!)

I am always surprised to find that many business owners look at everything in their business except the only thing that really matters at the end of the day for a for-profit entity: financial statements. Unfortunately, it seems that most business owners are a bit timid about looking at the financial reports, because they simply don't understand them at the level they would like. They only look at the easiest financial indicator they can get their hands on, which is the bank account balance, when in reality they need a much more robust tool like QuickBooks Online.

Unfortunately, this type of financial analysis does not work and leads companies of all sizes right into ruin. To be a successful entrepreneur and business owner, you must have a firm grasp of the basics of finances and accounting. I know what you are thinking. You want to skip this chapter because you think it is going to be boring, complicated, and will not add much value. But let me assure you that the contents in this chapter are going to be so easy to understand that you can hand the book to your twelve-year-old and have him or her start doing your financesfor you.

I don't mean to take a swipe at accountants, because I like them and they help me a great deal. At the same time, though, I almost believe that there is a global conspiracy to make entrepreneurs and business owners think accounting is a lot more complicated than it actually is in order to create job security for accountants. Everything you need to know can be explained in a few simple steps, and I will be outlining all of them for you in this chapter.

Stop driving with the windshield covered

There are three key documents that you must review on a monthly basis; without them, you are essentially driving your car with the windshield completely covered. Those three things have scary names, but I promise you, they are not scary at all once you learn how to read them.

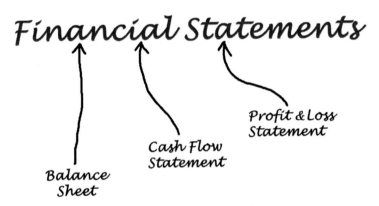

1. **Profit and loss statement** - In the next section, I will describe in detail how to read a profit and loss statement and how to get out of the habit of looking at just one number: the bottom line.
2. **Balance sheet** - I know this is a scary one. It's the one that most business owners are afraid of because they cannot seem to make sense of it, and I don't blame them. The way things are named on a balance sheet makes it essentially impossible to understand without twelveyears of education in accounting. But when you simplify things, as I will do for you, this document will become as easy to read as anything else.
3. **Statement of cash flows** - I know what you are thinking: *I have never heard of such a thing.* That's okay; most of you thought there were only two documents to look at, but there are actually three. This one is the most intuitive to read and understand, so it is one you will grasp quickly. But the point is to know how to use it.

To understand these three documents, it is critical to use them in unison. The reason there are three completely different documents is that each one tells a different story. In this chapter, I will explain to you what story each one tells so you can understand them on a deeper level. More importantly, I will tell you how to put the three different pieces of information together to do the only thing that matters when it comes to reading your financial statements: knowing the health of your company. This way if something's wrong, you'll know how to take the information you find in your financial statements and dig in to where you see issues.

Ultimate Financial Analysis Cheat Sheet

<u>Profit & Loss Statement</u>

1. **First Section** – Revenue
2. **Second Section** – Direct Costs
3. **Third Section** – Overhead Expenses
4. **Fourth Section** – Other Income & Expenses
5. **Fifth Section** – The Bottom Line

The top shows you the money you made, the middle is what you spent, and the bottom is what you theoretically have left over.

<u>Balance Sheet</u>

1. **Top Section**
   a. Current Assets
      i. Cash
      ii. Equipment
      iii. Inventory
      iv. Accounts Receivable
   b. Fixed Assets
      i. Property
      ii. Equipment
      iii. Other Fixed Assets

2. **Bottom Section**
   a. Liabilities
      i. Accounts Payable
      ii. Short-Term Debt (Credit Card Balances)
   b. Long-Term Liabilities
      i. Long-Term Debt
      ii. Deferred Income Tax

      iii. Other Long-Term Liabilities
- c. Equity
  - i. Owner's Capital
  - ii. Retained Earnings

The top and the bottom are always equal. They show all of the same things but from two different perspectives. The total of your assets will always equal the total of your liabilities plus your equity. If you have a lot of asses and very few liabilities, then you have a lot more equity in the company.

Cash Flow Statement

1. Cash flows from **Operating** Activities
2. Cash flows from **Investing** Activities
3. Cash flows from **Financing** Activities
4. **Supplemental** Information

The first one shows you money coming in and out from regular business activities, while the others show you activities relating to other parts of the business that are not from operations.

How to read and understand a profit and loss statement

Your profit and loss statement (P&L) is the document you are probably most familiar with. After all, this is the document that gives you "the bottom line." Unfortunately, what people didn't tell you before they handed you your profit and loss statement is that a P&L is almost entirely theoretical. This means that what you see on your P&L is not actually reality. It is a theoretical look at how your business could possibly be doing. There are a lot of assumptions made, and while this is an extremely useful document and it would be impossible to run a successful business without looking at it, it's important to understand that the numbers on the sheet are purely theoretical.

There are two ways your P&L can be set up and it all depends on how you or your accountant chose to set things up when you started your business. Most businesses are set up on an accrual basis, while other businesses are set up on a cash basis. For the remainder of this chapter, I will assume that your business is set up on an accrual basis. But if you are set up on a cash basis, don't worry. Most everything I say still applies to you with some very minor changes.

In order to massively simplify these systems, I am going to use terms that are not "official accounting" terms. Please forgive me for doing this. It is not because I don't understand how accounting works. Instead, it is because I have spent a lifetime simplifying complicated things. One of the ways I choose to simplify things is by getting rid of the fancy terms that people with fancy degrees have created. I do the same thing with the fancy terms in my field of neuroscience. While I am very proud of the degrees that hang on my wall, I don't need to use big words to make people think I am smarter than they are.

In the same way, I will not use many of the terms that your accountant might use to talk to you about your financial statements. Instead, I will use simple terms that make sense to all of us, and both you and your accountant will understand them upon hearing them for the first time.

One way a P&L can beset up is as follows:

ABC Company, Inc.	Profit & Loss Statement	February, 2016
Operating Revenue		
Product Sales		$25,000.00
Service Sales		$30,000.00
Total Operating Revenue		$55,000.00
Operating Expenses		
Cost of Goods sold		$10,000.00
Other Direct Costs		$2,000.00
Gross Profit		$43,000.00
Overhead		
Rent		$2,000.00
Insurance		$500.00
Office Supplies		$250.00
Utilities		$150.00
Overhead Payroll		$3,000.00
Other overhead		$100.00
Total Overhead		$6,000.00
Operating Income		$37,000.00
Other Income (Expenses)		
Loan Interest		($2,000.00)
Earning Before Income Taxes		$35,000.00
Income Taxes		$5,500.00
Net Earnings		$29,500.00

First Section: **Revenue**

This section of your P&L shows you the amount of money you have theoretically earned in this time period. Assuming you are looking at a month, this section shows you how much revenue (sales, gross sales) you have generated. There are two important parts I want to point out here.

1. This is not how much money you have actually made. Additionally, this is not how much profit you have made. This is simply

how much money you would theoretically have brought into your business if all of the customers you did business with paid all of their bills on time and handed you over a wad of cash every time you made a sale in the past month. If you're running your business on a cash basis, though, this is actually the amount of money you made.

2. This number is a "gross" number, which means it does not consider any expenses, costs, or overhead. Look at this number and make sure you realize that it is (1) theoretical and (2) does not consider costs. When this number is growing, it is often a very good thing. But be careful, because growing the "top line" without looking at the added costs and without considering the theoretical nature of this number can be disastrous for your business. Companies that traditionally focus on the top line typically find themselves in a very common predicament...grow, grow, gone!

In the example given here, ABC Company had a total of $55,000 in total operating revenue.

Second Section: **Direct Costs**

This middle section is all of the things related to directly doing the business you did to earn the revenues in the top section. This is essentially the direct cost of doing business. The key here is *direct*, and the importance of these numbers is that if you increase your top line, you will certainly increase the costs in this section. These are the costs directly associated with doing business.

For example, if you are in a retail business, things such as the cost of the items you sell will be included in this section. If you're in a service business, this number is a bit trickier but is typically all of the things that are directly related to doing more business. If you want to know if something should belong here, just consider: if you were to do 5% more business this month, would you need to do about 5% more of any one thing? If the answer is yes, then it goes in this section. If the answer is that you could probably get away with using the same resources you currently have in place, then it does not belong in this section and will go into the bottom section of your P&L.

The number at the bottom of this middle section represents your gross profit. It is called gross profit because your overhead has not yet been removed from this number. Therefore, things like your rent, utilities, and some of your biggest expenses are not considered here.

In the example given here, ABC Company had $12,000 in Operating Expenses, which left them with $43,000 in gross profit. At this point, you can also calculate the gross profit percentage or "gross margin" by doing the following math:
$43,000 / $55,000 = 0.782
Therefore, ABC Company had a gross margin of 78% for this period.

Third Section: **Overhead Expenses**

This section is essentially all of your overhead, or the costs that do not change as your business grows or shrinks to a certain extent. If you were to have a 10% increase in sales this month, this section should for the most part stay about the same. At the same time, if you were to have a slow sales month with 10% less in sales, again, this section should stay about the same.

Using a retail business as an example, you can see that whether you are in December, and having record-breaking sales, or you are in the month of May, which may be your slow month, the amount you pay for rent is probably exactly the same. Additionally, things like utilities will probably not change much, although extended hours during Christmas could potentially change this number slightly. Do not get focused on getting into the weeds of what goes here. Just assume that the things here are those that do not change directly as your sales change.

There is no question that if your sales change more than a certain amount, you will need to do additional things like increase office or warehouse space. Alternatively, if you have a significant slowdown in your business, you can certainly downsize your office and make other cuts. But for the most part, these numbers are not dramatically affected by the day-to-day of your business.

In the example given here, ABC Company had a total of $6,000 in total overhead expenses, which leaves them with $37,000 in operating income.

Fourth Section: **Other Income & Expenses**

This section involves things that, for the most part, an accountant should mess around with, so I don't even want to address them here. It's good to get to know what that stuff is, but it is certainly not a requirement if you have a good accountant who can do these things for you. Just know that there are some "magical" things that happen in that section that can significantly affect your bottom line. So make sure your accountant explains to you what is going on there on a quarterly basis.

In the example given here, ABC Company had a total of $7,500 in other income and expenses with $2,000 in loan interest that was paid in addition to $5,500 in taxes paid.

Fifth Section: **The Bottom Line**

At the very bottom of your P&L, you have a number called the bottom line. This is a number that you are very familiar with, because it is the one you love looking at. Unfortunately, because it is theoretical and no one told you it was, it is the most misleading number in the world of accounting. But don't get me wrong; it is still probably the most important. The reason it's theoretical is that this number can look really good or really bad, depending on some theoretical things that could happen.

For example, if you make some sales but don't actually collect on them, this number still looks really good. On the other hand, if you have a normal sales month but you make some big purchases, this number can look arbitrarily really bad, even if those purchases are not being paid for immediately. Some of those purchases, while not assets you are going to write off over a period of years, are still things that are going to add value to your business over the period of several months or more. Therefore, you must look at this number with a lot of caution.

Typically, the best person to understand the reality of this number is the CEO, who understands the overall scope of the company – but only if he or she understands that this is a theoretical number. Congratulations! You have now learned one-third of everything you need to know about accounting to run a successful business. In the next two chapters, I will give you the other two-thirds and you will be well on your way to knowing financial systems for your company better than just about any other entrepreneur that you know.

With $55,000 in total operating revenue and all other expenses subtracted, this leaves them with $29,500 in net earnings. At this point, you can also calculate the net profit percentage or "net margin" by doing the following math:
$29,500 / $55,000 = 0.536
Therefore, ABC Company had a net margin of 54% for this period.

Know how to read a balance sheet

Small business owners...drum roll please...it's time to talk about the most dreaded document for any small business owner without seven-teenadvanced business degrees. Yes, my friends, it's time for us to talk about the dreaded balance sheet. But don't worry. Remember, I'm the guy who has simplified neuroscience down to the point that can I teach it at seminars with hundreds of people who actually have no clue that I am talking to them about neuroscience. In a similar way, I have managed to break business down for you into some of the smallest and simplest steps you could imagine.

A balance sheet is not a scary thing, my friends. In fact, once you learn how to read it, you will realize that all of the fancy and complicated stuff is just "accounting talk." There are only a few things you need to know about a balance sheet and then you'll realize just how incredibly simple this document is.

One, there are essentially two parts to a balance sheet: the top part and the bottom part. The top part has all of your assets. The bottom part has liabilities and equity, typically owner's equity. There's one critical thing you must know about your balance sheet and that is that the top part and bottom part must always equal exactly the same. If your assets do not exactly equal your liabilities and your owner's equity, something is wrong.

ABC Company, Inc.	Balance Sheet	February 29, 2016
Current Assets		
Cash		$20,000.00
Inventory		$15,000.00
Accounts Receivable		$10,000.00
	Total Current Assets:	**$45,000.00**
Fixed Assets		
Property		$12,500.00
Equipment		$30,000.00
Other Fixed Assets		$17,500.00
	Total Fixed Assets:	**$60,000.00**
Total Assets		**$105,000.00**
Current Liabilities		
Accounts Payable		$20,000.00
Credit Card Balances		$10,000.00
Other Current Payables		$5,000.00
	Total Current Assets:	**$35,000.00**
Long-Term Liabilities		
Long-Term Debt		$10,000.00
Deferred Income Tax		$5,000.00
Other Long-Term Liabilities		$2,500.00
	Total Current Assets:	**$17,500.00**
Equity		
Owner's Capital		$30,000.00
Retained Earnings		$22,500.00
	Total Current Assets:	**$52,500.00**
Total Liabilities & Equity		**$105,000.00**

So now I know what you're thinking. You're thinking, *well, assets must be good and liabilities must be bad. So as long as I maximize the amount of assets I have and minimize the amount of liabilities, I will be in really good shape.* Well, sort of. There are four typical things that go into your assets. While some of them are good, others are not so good if you are not careful. Let's look at the things that go under assets:

Top Section of the Balance Sheet: Assets

Current Assets
- **Cash**: This is obviously a very good thing to have and there's not much I need to say about it.
- **Inventory**: The value of any inventory that you have on hand would show here as well. This is one that can be tricky. Is it good to have a lot of inventory or bad? Well, it's good from the perspective that if you have a lot of inventory, it means you have things you can sell. But it can be very bad if your inventory is growing and especially if you're in an industry where inventory values typically are on the decline or you run the risk of having inventory that you cannot sell.
- **Accounts Receivable**: Now, accounts receivables are the trickiest one of all. Is it good to have people owe you money? Yes, as long as they pay. So while accounts receivables are good if the people who owe you money are going to pay, accounts receivables can be very bad and in fact extremely dangerous if they arefrom people who may or may not pay, or may not pay on time. This is the number that can really trick you, and it is the one you should be looking at regularly any time you look at your profit and loss statement tosee ifyou've had a good month. Look at the bottom line and get a big smile on your face.

Fixed Assets
- **Property**: This is obviously a very good thing to have and there's not much I need to say about it.
- **Equipment**: This is the value of the equipment you own. It's important to mention at this point that if you purchased equipment but you took a loan on it, the loan would appear in the bottom half of this document. But the equipment value itself appears here.
- **Other Fixed Assets**: Other things including fancy accounting things like "accumulated depreciation" and things that you should mostly leave in the hands of your CPA for now.

I suggest holding onto that smile for just a few minutes and looking at your balance sheet and statement of cash flows. One of the first places I would look is at your accounts receivables, and not just looking at them from one point in time, but looking at how it has changed during that time period. If you are increasing in accounts receivables, that means more and more people owe you money. If some of this debt that people owe to you starts to get older and stale, especially over ninety days, you run the risk of never being able to collect on it, so proceed with caution. When you add up all of those numbers, you get your total assets, which completes the top portion of your balance sheet. Congratulations, my friends, you are now 50% of the way through learning how to read a balance sheet.

Bottom Section of the Balance Sheet: Liabilities and Equity

Current Liabilities:
- **Accounts Payable**: The first type of liability is accounts payable to your supplies. Now, accounts payable seems like a bad thing, but not always. Consider that if you owe someone money, it means that they've rendered some services to you or you bought some products from them, but you have yet to pay them. This is actually kind of a good thing from a cash flow perspective. As I said, it is not always that you want to have high assets and low liabilities, because that is not always the best situation for a company to be in. If in one month your assets significantly increase while your liabilities significantly decrease, that could spell disaster for most companies as it can lead to massive cash flow issues, which you will be able to read better after you learn how to read a statement of cash flows in the next section.
- **Credit Card Balances**: These are pretty obvious—they are money that you owe on credit cards.
- **Long-Term Debt**:This includes loans you have that you are paying back that are not accounts payable to suppliers and are not under credit cards. The total of these three items are all of your liabilities. The difference between your total liabilities and your total assets, therefore, is the owner's equity, which is the number that appears just below your total liabilities.

Long-Term Liabilities:
- **Long-Term Debt**: Longer term loans.
- **Deferred Income Tax**: Temporary differences between the company's accounting and actual taxes (leave it to your CPA).
- **Other Long-Term Liabilities**: Anything else (leave it to your CPA).

Equity:
- **Owner's Capital**: For a sole proprietorship, this would be the book value of the company.
- **Retained Earnings**: Company earnings that have not been paid out to the ownership.

I want to congratulate you. You now understand exactly what a balance sheet is. Do not let the fancy names, words like credits and debits, and the scariness of this document fool you. It is a very simple document that shows you on top what assets you have and shows you what liabilities you have in the bottom. Of course, again, the key to reading this effectively is to not think of assets as being good and liabilities as being bad. Just think of assets as being, well, assets and liabilities as being, well, liabilities. Realize that sometimes assets are good but occasionally they can be bad, while sometimes liabilities are bad but sometimes they can be good.

The key is to know how much you have in assets and liabilities and also understanding that a balance sheet is a snapshot in time. While the profit and loss statement gives you activity over a period of time, such as a month, a quarter, or a year, a balance sheet is simply a snapshot taken on a specific day at a specific time. It does not represent a range in time. So, often looking at the changes in your balance sheet from one time period to the next can be some of the most eye-opening information you can find.

Know how to read a statement of cash flows

We are now two-thirds of the way through understanding financial statements, but there is one more piece to learn, and that is the statement of cash flows. This is the one that for whatever reason, most accountants don't even print for the CEO. Furthermore, most CEOs don't know to ask for it. But in reality, it is one of the most important things you need to be look at. You should not be looking at a P&L and a balance sheet without looking at this document, because those first two documents can fool you into thinking business is good when it might not be good at all.

The first and most important thing to understand about a statement of cash flows is that, just like a P&L, it is for a period of time. But unlike a P&L, it is not based in theory. Instead, it is based in reality and the actuality of money flowing in and out of your company. But be careful when I say this is actuality and a P&L is theoretical. Even though this is the reality and your P&L shows you theory, often you can have your cash flow look pretty bad while your P&L looks pretty good. Also, while it may be bad for the given month, a strong P&L could indicate that your business is headed in the right direction, but not always. The key is to understand again that these three documents must be looked at together, and it is only when you consider all three at once that you can truly see what is happening in your business.

So let's look at the four different parts of this document.

ABC Company, Inc.	Statement of Cash Flows	February, 2016
Cash flow from operating activities		
Net Income		$18,000.00
Depreciation/Amortization		$2,000.00
Changes in operating accounts		$1,500.00
	Net cash provided by operating activities:	**$21,500.00**
Cash flow from investing activities		
Capital expenditures		($5,000.00)
proceeds from sale of equipment		$0.00
other investment activities		$0.00
	Net cash provided by investing activities:	**($5,000.00)**
Cash flow from financing activities		
Paying long-term debt		($2,000.00)
Other financing activities		$0.00
	Net cash provided by financing activities:	**($2,000.00)**
Other supplemental information		
Other cash flow items		$0.00
	Net cash provided by other activities:	**$0.00**
Beginning Cash		**$5,500.00**
Ending Cash		**$20,000.00**
Increase (Decrease) in Cash		**$14,500.00**

Section #1: Cash flow from operating activities

Operating activities are basically the things that appear on your P&L. While the P&L looks at the theory of how much money you are spending or making, this section of the statement of cash flows looks at how much money has actually come in and gone out. So, while a P&L might look at how much sales you theoretically made to a customer, this document looks at how much that customer actually paid you. While a P&L assumes that you have a certain amount to pay for rent every month, this document only considers that amount if you pay your rent.

If one month you skip rent and in another month you pay additional rent, this document will show you exactly what you actually spent, not what you would have spent theoretically.

Section #2: Cash flow from investing activities

This is all of the things that you do that relate to investing in equipment and other activities. For example, if you purchase or sell equipment, this is the section that those expenditures and proceeds would go into. This can be confusing for some business owners, but it's important to understand that if you sell something you own, such as a forklift, that is not considered operating income because you are not in the business of buying and selling forklifts. Therefore, you have taken an asset and sold it. So on a statement of cash flows, it will show up in this section and on your balance sheet accordingly. But that sale will not show up on your profit and loss statement, which is why you cannot look at just your profit and loss statement.

Section #3: Cash flow from financing activities

This is money that has to do with payments on long-term debt, proceeds from stock, dividends, and things like that. This is a section that most small business owners should not concern themselves with much at first, but it can become important as a company grows.

Section #4: Other supplemental information

This section can include some other supplemental information such as the exchange of significant items that did not involve cash, and it also reports the amount of income taxes paid as well as interest paid.

Some statements of cash flows will also make it simple for you by showing the beginning cash and ending cash, which allows you to see how much money you started off with, how much money you ended with, and what the difference was. A positive cash flow means that more cash came into the business than went out, while a negative cash flow means that you had less cash coming in than going out. As a reminder, do not be fooled by thinking this means you had a good or bad month. It is just one report out of three that you must analyze to get the entire picture.

Now I want to congratulate you. You have officially graduated with more knowledge about understanding financial statements than most people understand after years of business school. These three documents are all you need to know about your business' finances, and to make it easy, I've given a summary of everything you need to know about them below.

The profit and loss statement is simply a theory of how your business is doing. The first portion shows you the revenue that you are theoretically generating, the second portion shows you your cost of doing business in theory, and the third section shows you your overhead expenses in theory. At the very bottom of that document, you see how much money you theoretically may have made or lost.

Your balance sheet then shows how many assets and liabilities you have and it has two main sections, which should always add up to be the same number. The top half shows your assets, including things like cash, equipment, inventory, and accounts receivable. The bottom half shows liabilities, such as accounts payable to suppliers, credit cards, and long-term debt, in addition to owner's equity.

Finally, your statement of cash flows shows you how much cash is flowing in and out of your company in the form of operating activities, investing activities, and financing activities, and it also shows you how much cash you started and ended the period with. With this information in hand, I would suggest that you go right now and run a profit and loss statement, balance sheet, and a statement of cash flows for your company for a recent period so you can see this information in real time for a real company you understand.

If you do not currently have a business and are not able to do this, then I suggest you create yourself a pretend business, such as a lemonade stand, and take yourself through some sort of a game that allows you to put this information to use. All this information is extremely easy to understand. If you do not use it immediately, you will forget it. So go put it to use and congratulations on officially knowing more about accounting than 98% of entrepreneurs anywhere in the world today.

Questions every business owner should be able to answer

P&L Analysis
1. What's the Top Line? (Total revenue or sales).
2. What's the Gross Profit? (Money you made after direct costs but before overhead).
3. What's the Gross Margin? (Percentage of the money you made that you sort of get to keep).
4. What's the Bottom Line? (Amount of money you sort of made, in theory, if everyone paid you and you paid everyone immediately and a bunch of other assumptions).
5. What's the Net Profit Margin? (Percentage of the money you made that you theoretically get to keep).

Balance Sheet
1. How much cash do you have?
2. How much do you own in equipment?
3. How much inventory do you have?
4. How much money do people owe you?
5. How much money do you owe people?
6. How much do you owe on credit cards and other short-term debt?
7. How much do you owe in long-term debt?
8. How much equity do you have sitting in the company?

Cash Flow Statement
1. How much cash came in from doing business?
2. How much cash came in (or out) from things you invested in?
3. How much cash came in (or out) from things you financed?
4. What else affected cash balances?
5. How much cash did you start the month with?
6. How much cash did you end the month with?
7. What was the net gain or loss of cash?

Reality Check – Time to be CEO
1. Notice what doesn't look right and go figure out why it happened the way it did.
2. Notice what is not similar to the last period and find out why.
3. Notice if the numbers for the Bottom Line and Net Gain of cash seem in line.
4. If the bottom line and net gain do not coincide, dig to find out why.

Chapter X

Revolutionize Your Industry or Perish

No industry is static. In order for a business to not only grow but even to survive, it must be in a state of constant evolution. Growth and evolution come from one thing and one thing alone: innovation. The most successful businesses in the world are constantly evolving and innovating in order to reach the next level and ensure that they are not left behind. As your business gains strength from its experience and authority, you must also realize that there is also a tendency for complacency and stagnation.

The world is changing all around us. With the digital revolution encompassing our lives, the world is changing at a rate that we have never seen before. To remain competitive and stay at the top of your industry, you must constantly be innovating and pushing the envelope to take your business and yourself to a new level.

Don't just run a business—revolutionize an industry

If you're in business to compete and be at the top of your industry, you are playing the wrong game. Instead of just being in the business and doing whatever everyone else does, I challenge you to instead revolutionize your entire industry. Think differently than everyone else in your industry. Think bigger. Think faster. Think smarter. Think better. Revolutionize your industry by offering your clients results that are unlike what any other competitor can possibly deliver.

Get to know your customers' pain points and focus on how to annihilate them. When you look at a company like Apple and think of what Steve Jobs did, you realize that the man was responsible for revolutionizing at least six completely different industries. If you think of what he did with the cell phone, he realized that everyone was building flip phones and competing to see who can make the best one. Instead of competing with them, Steve Jobs quietly laughed at them and set out to completely revolutionize the cellular phone industry. He did something that, in a few short years, allowed Apple to become the largest company in the world.

At the same time, it took Apple from a company that had no market share in the cell phone industry to one that absolutely dominated every competitor. Steve Jobs and Apple did the same thing with the tablet, the music industry, and the portable music player industry, not to mention the desktop computer industry and possibly a few others.

You can then look at an example of a company like Tesla. In this company, Elon Musk has not just built an electric vehicle; he has in fact completely revolutionized the auto industry. As I write this portion of my book, I am traveling on the freeway, speaking into a recording device while my car drives itself. While I am still supposed to have my eyes on the road and my hands on the steering wheel, the car is accelerating and decelerating on its own, and steering itself in order to stay perfectly between the lane markings. As I write this portion, the car in front of me has slowed down to about 46 mph and my car has quietly done the same. As he is now starting to speed up and pull away, my car is speeding up along with him.

In addition to this, when I got into my car just a few moments ago, my car had already turned on and the temperature was set to the approximate setting I like in the early morning hours. I did not have to tell the car to do this, nor did I have to click one button. Instead, my car knows that every morning at approximately 4:00 a.m., I get in and drive away. It also knows that I like to set the temperature at somewhere around 73 degrees. So instead of it waiting for me to get in the car, it does all of this automatically, knowing that this is my usual plan. It also knows my typical routes, so when I get in the car at the office towards the end of the day, it brings up my home address on the navigation panel and asks me if I want to take the typical route or choose another it has found for me that might have less traffic.

These are just a few of the innovations that Elon Musk has brought into the auto industry. But the most impressive innovation of all is that I don't know what my Tesla Model S will offer me tomorrow. Every once in awhile as I lie sleeping in my bed, my car sits in my garage, connected to the Wi-Fi in my house, and communicates with the geniuses back at Tesla, who are planning their next big upgrade.

One time when I got in my car, it notified me that it had upgraded itself and it could now go from zero to 60 mph in 3.0 seconds, instead of 3.2 seconds. Another time, it told me that it can now parallel park and drive itself. Yet another time, it simply told me that there were upgrades made to the navigation. Those are examples of true innovation. Elon Musk and the folks at Tesla have completely revolutionized the auto industry. But as I write this book, the world doesn't know it yet.

The same was true in 2007, when we didn't realize that we would ALL be using iPhones very soon. What most people don't know yet is that we will ALL be driving a Tesla soon. I know what some of you are thinking as you read this book; you think to yourself that you don't have an iPhone. Instead, you have a Samsung or some other sort of Android or Microsoft device. Let's not kid ourselves. Whether your phone says Samsung, Motorola, Microsoft, Android, or anything else, it is still in your hands only because of the innovations made by Apple and Steve Jobs in 2007. In fact, your Android device is an iPhone, just a different model of it. In ten years, you will be driving a Tesla. It may or may not be electric and it may or may not have a Tesla logo on it, but I can assure you that in ten years, all of us will be driving Elon Musk's innovations.

So now that you have heard the stories of these amazing entrepreneurs who have revolutionized entire industries, think to yourself, *what is the innovation in my industry that is missing? What can I do that is revolutionary? How can I take my industry and company to levels that have ever been seen before?* Answer these questions with the goal to do something that has never been done before, and strive to be the best you can possibly be and make your company the best it can possibly be. Revolutionize an industry and you will not only watch your profits soar, but you will see just how enjoyable it is to start having fun with what you do.

Always start with best practices

You are correct; I love innovation. But there are two things I like even more than innovation: research and observation. Before you can innovate and revolutionize anything, the key is to first learn and understand the best practices within your industry. Observe what others are doing that works. Research the best ways to get the results that you want to get for your clients, and learn how to apply the best practices and all of the research within your business first. Once you have done this and have set up an infrastructure that is as good as anyone else's in the industry, it is time to begin innovating.

If Apple had designed the most incredible touch screen in the world but it had failed to make a phone which could make clear-sounding phone calls, no one would have cared about the touchscreen or the fancy features. In the same manner, if Elon Musk had built a car that could drive itself but didn't have the basic functionality of a car, no one would be interested in driving one.

In every industry, there are a set of best practices and there are companies that do things extremely well. Even if you don't feel that they are doing things extremely well, there are certain companies that are doing things better than everyone else. Your job is to first find out what they are doing that works. Research the best practices and document them in a way that you can utilize within your own business. Focus on learning what works, not just what sounds good, because the most important thing is getting results for your clients and solving their pain points.

There are many ways of finding best practices within an industry. One simple way is to search online. You will be amazed at the wealth of knowledge there is on the internet. Another way is to talk to people who have worked in some of the best companies in your industry. Another is to attend the top conferences and learn from what they have to say there. You can of course read magazines, watch videos, and read books as well. But the key is to do whatever you can to gain insights on the best practices that are already available.

Once you have created your baseline of the best practices within your industry, it is time for you to prepare for innovation.

Revolutionize and blow them out of the water

By now, you have identified and learned the best practices in the industry, and you have observed and conducted significant research into figuring out how to make sure you're not missing out on any advantage that your competitors may already have. On top of that, you are innovating and focusing on revolutionizing the industry, so you are set to blow the competition out of the water.

You see, when a company establishes a solid foundation by implementing best practices from their industry, as well as industries that are comparable, and then layers innovation on top of it, it sets you up to do things for your customers that others are simply not able to do. When you address customer pain points at this level, it makes everything you do significantly easier. In fact, if you think about it, every aspect of your business becomes easier when you implement best practices and innovate on top of it.

For example, think about how much easier it is to do marketing when you are marketing a product or service that is truly revolutionary – one that is unique in the industry, going above and beyond what anyone else is doing. Then think of your sales process. Imagine how much easier it is to make sales when your presentation can clearly state that you are not only doing everything that everyone else is doing (which is a best practice), but you are doing the things that no one else can come close to doing. It is these simple practices that are going to make every step of the process easier.

Suddenly, you are marketing and selling better than ever before. In addition, by implementing best practices, your operational controls are unlike what anyone else has. And of course, your customers and employees are more than just satisfied; they are truly raving fans of your organization. The numbers on your KPI dashboard look great and you are excited to look at them on a daily basis. Innovation can cause just about every other aspect of your business to flourish.

Above all, when you are innovating, it creates a fun atmosphere for you to work in. You can go to work every day feeling like you are having fun — not just showing up to work. Every day, you can be proud of what you are helping to create and build within your organization. For these and other reasons, I recommend that you innovate consistently. Imagine the day when you are the Apple of your industry. You may already be there, and if you are, congratulations. You know how good it feels. If you are not already there, don't worry. Becoming the Apple of your industry is not as far away as you may think. Start focusing on innovation today and enjoy blowing the competition completely out of the water.

Chapter XI

The Ultimate Secret

We have been through quite a journey together, you and I. At this point, you have the tools and the skills that I have used to grow over a dozen companies. These are the same tools I have used to help hundreds and thousands of business owners massively improve their companies. In most cases, my clients have doubled profits in less than six months by applying these principles.

Of course, the key is that these principles are only effective if you actually apply them. While I would like to hope that you are going to apply everything that I teach in this book, I understand that the reality is most business owners will not apply anymore than 25% to 50% of these in the short term.

The good news, however, is that my clients who have doubled profits in six months or less using these principles have not applied every one of them, and you don't need to either. In fact, while I don't keep track of exactly what percentage of my tools each client actually applies, I can tell you that the number for even the most successful business owners is somewhere around 25% – at most. What that means is that these tools are so powerful that even applying just a small portion of them will massively improve your business.

The key is for you to determine which of these are going to have the biggest impact on your bottom line, and apply those first and foremost. Read these last few sections and get ready to inject rocket fuel into your business.

Beat the sun out of bed

Young entrepreneurs always ask me about the one secret that could help them massively improve their business. When most ask me that question, they are looking for me to tell them some secret formula. But in reality, I tell them that the single biggest change you can make within your organization to massively increase your revenues, profits, and the quality of services you provide is to work harder than you've ever worked before.

Now I understand you do not intend on working your butt off for the rest of your life. However, I do want you to understand that no one has achieved anything of greatness in the history of mankind without truly working hard. As I have interviewed, observed, and read about the most successful entrepreneurs in the history of mankind, and in fact, the most successful people in the history of mankind, including athletes, political leaders, and entrepreneurs, there is one thing that they all seem to have in common. That is simply that they all consistently work harder than everyone else around them.

As I write this section of the book, it is 5:57 a.m. my time. I am here writing this section of the book while all of my two hundred plus employees in six-plus companies are still either sleeping or at home. While many of them are salaried and could already be at the office, they are not. Additionally, I have already put in two and a half hours by the time I am done writing this sentence. I have already been to the gym and worked out. I have answered about fiftyemails. I have completed a few tasks which required my attention in the early morning hours, and I am now here writing this content for you.

Throughout my life, I have worked harder than anyone I have ever known. While people have insulted me by calling me a "genius" at various stages in my life, I know that I am anything but a genius. At times, I have been insulted in other ways by being referred to as "talented," but once again, I know that I am anything but. Talent is just a word we like to use to label the hardworking, because we cannot comprehend or fathom just how much hard work it takes to succeed. We label them as talented to justify our own lazy behavior. In fact, I truly believe that genius is a lifetime of effort put forth in private for a few moments of seemingly effortless results in public.

We see Olympians who dazzle an entire stadium with their performance that starts and ends in less than sixty seconds. As we watch in awe, we think of just how talented they are and how easy they make it look. What most of us forget is that for the last twelve years of their life or more, they have gotten out of bed earlier than any one of their friends and any one of their family members. They have worked harder than probably anyone else, not only in their family and their group of friends, but probably anyone else in their entire sport. As they stand on that podium to accept a gold medal, we forget the path and the journey they have taken to get there.

We forget their performance at the last Olympics four years ago, where they had worked harder than ever before and didn't even make their way to the podium. We forget the Olympics four years before that, where they didn't even qualify to compete, and watched it on television with the rest of us. We forget that four years before that, as the other children played outside or slept, this personwas up and practicing their art.

Therefore, it is easy to look at some of the most successful entrepreneurs we have seen such as Steve Jobs, Bill Gates, Elon Musk, Mark Zuckerberg, and many before them and think that they are geniuses, or just talented. We forget that regardless of the industry they were in or what companies they started, they all had one thing in common, and that is that they worked harder than anyone else around them. So, today my message to you is this: if you want to succeed, you are going to need to put a lot of hard work into a lot of skills.

I have outlined tenof those most important strategies in this book, but know that all of those strategies are useless without the eleventh strategy and the most important tool of all: hard work. I challenge you join me on this journey where every morning, we beat the sun out of bed and start our day in a manner that allows us to give more to the universe than could have ever been expected of us. The journey of life is not long. Sadly, it comes and goes in the blink of an eye, from what I've been told. Even one hundredyears on this planet is nowhere near enough for any of us to do everything that we want. So let's not squander those few valuable moments that we have.

Every morning, dare the sun to beat you out of bed. Challenge the sun to get up before you. And every morning as you get up hours before the sun has opened its eyes, look outside at the black skies and remind yourself that once again, you have beat the sun out of bed. Just as the sun sleeps while you work, your competitors sleep while you grow. You will realize that in life and in business, you only truly have one competitor: yourself. If you can learn to manage that one competitor and keep yourself performing at your peak, I can assure you that in life, in business, and in love, you will have no other competitors and no worthy opponent. I'm reminded of a great quote from Mark Cuban: "Work like there is someone working 24 hours a day to take it away from you."

I ask you to chant with me as we tell the universe the reality of what is. I am not the smartest nor am I the most talented. I was certainly not handed the most ideal situation to succeed. But I will work harder than anyone else I know and I will work harder than anyone could expect of me in order to use the gifts that God has blessed me with to leave a mark on this Earth, to leave the universe a better place than I found it. I will take this opportunity and I will use it to make myself and the world a better place.

So as we inch closer to the ending of this book, I want you focused on the most important element I have taught you, and that is that nothing worth achieving has ever been achieved without hard work. Hard work trumps everything else.

Ask for failure

Throughout the chapters of this book, I have shared many secrets with you. On multiple occasions, I have told you that if the tools I share with you are utilized, I can guarantee you results. In reality, I can never truly guarantee that anything I have taught you in this book is going to work as well for you as it does for others. But there is one guarantee I can make you that applies to every reader of this book, regardless of what business you are in, how long you've been in business, what industry you are trying to dominate, what country you live in, and anything else that makes you different from other people reading this book.

That simple fact is that before you succeed, you must and you will fail many times. In fact, in order to succeed, you must learn to not only deal with failure but learn how to embrace it. And if you truly want to inject your business with rocket fuel, you must learn to ask for failure.

Now be careful when I say to ask for failure. I am not suggesting that you make poor decisions and act lazy so that you fail. I am simply encouraging you to push the limits and dare the universe to allow you to fail. The only way you can actually grow and get to the next level is by pushing the limits of what you are comfortable doing. Anytime you push the limits of your comfort, you are going to fail many more times than you will succeed.

But failure can become just one of the routine steps on your path to ultimate success. As children, we embrace failure and we dare the universe to make us fail. In fact, children will push the limits of what they can do consistently without giving up until they achieve the results they are after. Imagine just how much effort it takes for a child to learn to crawl. If you have never had an infant in your home, you would be amazed that any time you place an infant on their belly, they begin to struggle to crawl, even if they are tired or nowhere near prepared to actually crawl. At some point, they may cry or scream and they may throw a tantrum, but they will never give up on trying.

Interestingly enough, soon after they learn to crawl, instead of being perfectly satisfied with crawling and considering themselves an expert crawler, a child is programmed to then attempt to walk. So the next six months to one year of their lives is spent learning how to walk. Once again, they fail over and over and over again. But with each failure, they get one step closer to taking their first step. They do not give up, sit in a corner, and proclaim that they simply are not talented enough to walk or that they just don't want to be one of those "walkers."

Instead, they get up and try to walk. As parents and adults around them, we encourage them to do so by clapping and cheering for them every time they try to take a step. When they take a half step and fall right down on their butts, we don't point at them and say, "You are a failure." They don't look at themselves as a failure, either. Instead, they put a big grin on their face and we all clap for them and cheer the fact that they have graduated to the next level and are now capable of taking half a step.

So if we have this beautiful system built within us as human beings, then why do we struggle so much to embrace failure as adults? Why do we assume that success must come without a multitude of failures? Why is it that we don't consider a half a step, followed by falling on our face or butts, as a success? Why do our family and friends stop cheering for us when we try and fail? And why do we give up after a while?

Sadly, it is because the human body was not designed to live one hundredyears. When you look at the history of mankind, human beings are designed to live somewhere around a maximum of thirtyyears. Therefore, just about everything in our bodies begins to fall apart by the age of thirtyor even earlier. In fact, the simplest of functions within our bodies cease to work at a certain age because our bodies were never designed to last that long. But through modern medicine and the heroism of scientists all around the world, we are now able to enjoy life on this planet for a century or even more if we take good care of our bodies.

But keep in mind that your mind and body begin to "fall apart" by the time you're in your mid-twenties. This can be seen best in professional athletes who typically reach their peak somewhere in their twenties and then have a slow decline. As I write this book, the man who has been the icon of Los Angeles basketball for two decades, Kobe Bryant, is in his last year as an NBA player. As we watch him get out there and work hard every day, we see that he is not anything close to what he was at his prime. The man is only in his late thirties.

So what does our bodies falling apart and athletes have to do with you as a businessperson, and how does this all relate to failure? The way it relates is that as children and young adults, we embrace failure and we push the limits. But as we get older, something inside of us begins to prepare us for death. Somewhere in our twenties, our bodies and minds "decide" that instead of trying to be better and better every day, we are better off just being comfortable. After all, we are almost dead anyways.

But in today's society, where you may live seventy-five years past your twenty-fifth birthday, this is a horrible approach to life! Knowing this, you must get up every morning before the sun comes up and be ready to battle. Be prepared to embrace life. Be prepared to embrace failure and to ask for it. Dare the universe to allow you to fail, because you know that with each failure, you are one step closer to the ultimate goal.

Dare the universe to give you a challenge big enough that you are not capable of overcoming, because soon, you will learn to grow and you will overcome the challenges that you could not overcome yesterday. Tomorrow, you will be a better man or woman than you are today, as long as you are willing to embrace failure.

I know a lot of people and I have a pretty large family. I love my friends, my family members, and my colleagues who have been with me for so many years. I can tell you that some of them are smarter than me, some of them are taller than me, and some are shorter than me. Some are bigger than me and some are smaller than me. Some have lighter skin, while others have darker skin. Some have more experience and some have less experience. Some are older and some are younger. Some have more money and some have less.

But there is one thing I can tell you that, without a doubt, makes me head and shoulders different than anyone else in my family, in my circle of friends, and in people I know. I am by far the biggest failure I know. I do not have a KPI dashboard to compare me to my friends and family, so I can't give you exact numbers, but I can tell you that I can't imagine anyone around me who has ever failed as many times as I have. I have failed in every aspect of life. I have failed in sports, in love, in friendship, in school, in business...oh yes, I have failed many times in business.

Growing up as a kid in Los Angeles and being a die-hard Lakers fan who loves Magic Johnson and Kobe Bryant, it's hard for me to admit that the greatest player to ever play the game of basketball is Michael Jordan. But after a quarter of a century of battling that thought, I am willing to admit publicly in this book that Michael Jordan is the greatest player to have ever played the game. After reading this quote from him, I am thinking that he may be the best who will ever play the game.

Michael Jordan said, "I've missed more than 9,000 shots in my career. I've lost almost 300 games. Twenty-six times, I've been trusted to take the game-winning shot and missed. I've failed over and over and over again in my life. And that is why I succeed."

When I read that quote for the first time, I was in awe. I felt like someone had gone into my heart and mind and had extracted my thoughts and feelings. There was an overwhelming feeling of joy knowing that I was not alone in being a failure.

Since then, I have learned to recognize that failure is the biggest type of triumph we can have as human beings and as entrepreneurs. So I challenge you to do as I have: I challenge you to go out and fail. Fail over and over again, but fail because you pushed the limits, not because you didn't try hard enough. There's a big difference between failure as a result of action and failure as a result of inaction. Be the entrepreneur who fails because you pushed the limits. Fail because you expected more of yourself than anyone else. Fail because you embraced things no one else would embrace. Fail because you are hungry. Fail because you are adventurous. Fail you because you are daring. But do not fail because you are lazy.

Go out there today and dare the world to give you failure.

The Ultimate Secret to mastering business

We've been on an incredible journey together and have gone through a quarter of a century of business experience, which I shared with you throughout the pages of this book. I've encouraged you to work hard, embrace failure, and even beat the sun out of bed in the morning. You've learned a little bit of just how hard I work and how I strive every day to be a better businessman than I was the day before. This next part is going to come as a bit of a surprise to most readers.

I want you to know that I do not think that business is, by any stretch of the imagination, the most important thing in life. In fact, there is no "most important thing in life." By definition, you cannot consider any one thing to be significantly more important than everything else, because everything in life works together in a beautiful balance. As you read this, some of you will argue that family is above everything else and that is the most important thing. I would like to agree with you, but what would your family mean if you don't have health or if they don't have good health?

But is health the most important thing? Well, what good is good health without having your family, friends, and the people you love all around you? What about emotional health – being happy, enjoying life, and having fun? Should those just be ignored? After all, what good is having a great family and being in extremely good health if you are not happy?

At the same time, how can you provide for the family you love so much if your career and your mission are not performing at the level you expect? Take it one step further and even ask: what if you have all the money in the world, a wonderful family, good health, and you have lots of fun, but you are not contributing to society? Where does that leave you in the long run? Regardless of your spiritual beliefs, you must believe that every one of us has some sort of a spirit. And if you think by spirit, I am referring to a mystical, transparent cutout that floats out of your body, remember that I am a neuroscientist. Spirits could mean many things that go well beyond a ghost.

So what would life be like if you are not contributing? How can you contribute if you don't have the financial means? And how can you have the financial means if your business is not thriving? If your business is not thriving, can you truly have fun and can you truly have emotional health and happiness? What about your physical health? Can you truly be physically healthy if you are not taking care of yourself by watching what you eat and making sure that you take care of your body by exercising regularly?

The answer is that there truly is no hierarchy in life of what is more important than everything else. In my humble opinion, life is like a wheel and everything has the same level of importance. Each part of the wheel supports the rest of it, and when any part is not functioning properly, the wheel as a whole does not function at its maximum potential.

For our entire lives, people have tried to tell us what it means to be successful. Some of you had parents like mine who told me that in order to be successful, I must be a doctor or a lawyer. Others were influenced more by theirpeers who told themthat success meant being cool and having the highestnumber of friends. Regardless of what others have told you is the definition of success, I challenge you to create your own definition and stop living by the rules that other people have created for you, especially those that were created so many years ago and are now truly outdated. But you have been living by them for so long that you may have a hard time letting them go.

The Titanium Wheel of Life is simply a way to gauge where you feel you stand in ten different areas of life on a scale of one to ten. I do not know the definition of success and I would never dare tell someone else what I feel it means to be successful. So if you thought I would tell you that having a big, powerful company with massive profits makes you successful, you could not be further from the truth. I would never define success for anyone, including my own children and even you, someone who has invested in purchasing my book.

All I can tell you is that my best guess at what it takes to be successful is balance. I feel that power and strength come from balance. I feel that success comes from balance. Now, typically, the people who say they want "balance" are those who are just trying to be lazy, and telling us they want balance is just their way of sleeping a little more than they should, watching more television than they should, and not spending enough time achieving their dreams. When asked why they have yet to achieve their dreams, they give the excuse that they want balance in their lives. They will say that they want "work-life balance" or something else like that.

The reality is that balance does not give you the excuse to be lazy. In fact, to truly have balance, you must strive to be more and to do more every day. Balance is the reason I am awake two to three hours before the sun comes up almost every day, because those two to three hours in the morning allow me to spend a little bit of extra time with my children at night. They allow me to have a bit more freedom to travel more with my wife. I encourage you to look at the Wheel of Life and complete this wheel by putting a line where you feel each area of your life is ranking on a scale of one to ten, with zero being worst and ten being the best. Don't be too hard on yourself and give yourself a realistic score of where you see the various aspects of your life as they are today, not as the way you would like to live.

For example, if you are not contributing to others and you are not donating your time, money, or anything else, but you really have a great heart and one day you want to save the world, you are still at a zero in contribution on the Wheel of Life. If you want to have great physical health, yet you eat processed food every day, drink soda, and you don't work out consistently, then don't fool yourself by giving yourself a seven. Be honest with yourself and complete this wheel, then take a good look at the wheel you create.

The Titanium Wheel of Life

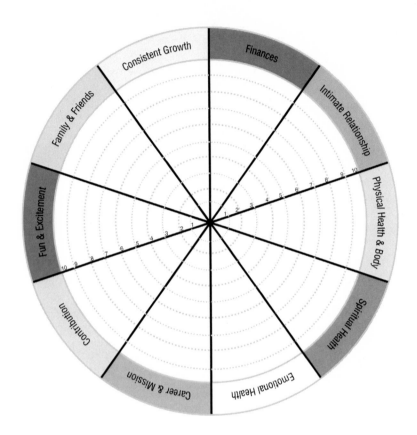

To create your own wheel, download the Titanium Life app and use the live wheel-generator. It even allows you to track your wheel over a period of time and share it with others.

Remember, the power in a wheel does not necessarily come from the size of the wheel, but instead from the balance that the wheel has. Imagine how well your car would drive if the four wheels on it were shaped like the wheel you have on this drawing. If you're anything like the thousands of people who attend my seminars and complete this as a group, you will look at it and realize that your car would not get very far with a wheel that looks like this. I ask you to then think how can you achieve everything you want in life if your wheel looks like this?

The good news is that it is very easy to change the way your wheel looks and it is very easy to master these ten areas of life. All it takes is consistent daily effort. You'll find that you don't need to scale anything back in order to address the areas that aren't going as well either. As your focus goes there, you might find that nothing suffers, but in some cases, you may have some minor setbacks as you learn to adjust.

Since many businesspeople and entrepreneurs suffer from not taking care of their health, I will take just one moment to talk to you about a simple way that you could improve your health. While I teach entire seminars on health and fitness and I have an upcoming book on the topic of health and fitness, I will give you the quickest and shortest version of this topic here in the next paragraph.

As a busy entrepreneur, all you need to understand to have incredible health and fitness is this:

1. You shape your body in the gym and you size your body in the kitchen. That means you cannot go to the gym to try to lose weight. In fact, I have a famous saying that is, "Say no to cardio," yet I keep in very, very good shape. Cardiovascular exercise is good for your body and your heart especially, but if you think that running on a treadmill for thirty minutes, an hour, or even two hours is going to give you health, you are unfortunately wrong. There are many reasons that this does not work, not the least of which is that it is not sustainable. Anything that you do in life that is not sustainable is not worth doing.

    So if you do not go to the gym to lose weight, then what do you do there? The gym is a place to shape your body and to build strength. If you do it correctly as a busy entrepreneur, you can follow my simple twenty-five-minute workout, which you can find on my website at titaniumsuccess.com, and where you will also find multiple workout regimens, videos, and even images that will guide you in this process. You can also find this on the Titanium Success app, found both in the iPhone App Store and on Android.

2. Go to the gym for only twenty-five minutes every day, but you must go three hundred and sixty-five days a year. That means you go to the gym on your birthday, on Christmas, and even on the days you are not feeling well. It doesn't matter how busy you are or what you've got going on; you always go to the gym. But

when you go, you are limited to being in there for only twenty-five minutes, so you had better get moving fast.

I have a twenty-five minute strength training routine that anyone can follow, from a beginner to a professional bodybuilder. This twenty-five minute routine allows you to do simple movements that will not only strengthen your muscles, but will also give you the cardiovascular exercise that you need, because you are moving consistently for twenty-five minutes.

3. In addition, you must realize that the kitchen is where you size your body. That means in order to lose weight and to be healthy, you are going to need to:

    a. Consume fewer calories.
    b. Consume less of the foods that are literally poisoning your body.

Some of the worst foods that instantaneously poison your body and cause you to gain weight are things like processed carbohydrates, including white bread, white rice, white pasta, sugary drinks, and anything that instantly injects sugar into your body. Again, if you download the Titanium Success App or you go to titaniumsuccess.com, you can find my nutrition guide, which divides all foods into four different categories. It gives you an easy way to figure out what you must stop eating, what you should limit, and what is okay to eat in moderation.

Of course, this is not a health book, so I will not go too much further down this tangent. But as an entrepreneur, I want you to take better care of your body. I also want you to take better care of your family. I want you to take better care of your health, your spirit, and make sure that you are having a good time and are happy. The most successful businesses in the world and all of the money in the world combined are nothing compared to happiness.

But at the same time, I don't want you to get me wrong. Money is not a bad thing; it is a very good thing to have, especially in the hands of good people. So, today as you finish this book, I encourage you to join me on my journey of creating a group of human beings who strive to be better every day. People who work hard to be the best that they can possibly be every day so that they can be happy and they can help other human beings by leading with their heart.

Apply the skills I have taught in this book and your business will grow in ways you cannot imagine. Before I leave you, I want you to know that I hope to meet you in person one day. And when I do, I look forward to you telling me how impactful this book has been on your life. I look forward to you telling me how you've shared this book and my message with dozens of other people. If you enjoyed this book, please don't forget to write me a review online and please don't forget to share these words with anyone else you think might need it.

I hope to meet you at one of my upcoming events. I am honored that you have spent this time with me and I am excited about the results you are going to see in your business in the coming weeks, months, and years. Before I leave you, I have prepared a 15-step action plan for success for you. Look at this list and apply these action items in your business, and watch it grow like never before.

Chapter XII

Shortcut to Doubling Your Profits in Six Months

Now that you know the secrets for supercharging your business, I want to share a shortcut with you that will help you make some big things happen in a short time. I have never been a patient person so the thought of working for decades to make something happen just does not get me motivate. That is why I created this easy to follow plan for doubling your company's profits in just six months.

Before you start this process, however, you must first make sure you are in the right industry. It doesn't matter how good your company is, how well you do marketing, and how hard you work if the industry you are in is dying. Take a step back, look at your industry, and determine if it is growing, maintaining, or shrinking. Do not waste a decade of your life building a company in an industry that is simply not lucrative. Once you know you're in the right industry, implement these fifteensecrets and enjoy the success that will follow.

Step #1: Track and measure results.

If you want to double your profits in six months, you must first start by knowing what your profits are now and track them on a regular basis. In most businesses, this can easily be done monthly. However, if you have a smaller business, you may even be able to track this more often, such as weekly. If you track your profit on a regular basis, you and your team will magically start doing new things that will increase revenue, cut costs, and increase profitability.

Action item: Place a one-hour weekly or monthly block on your calendar to review your company's profits, and do absolutely everything you can prior to this block to make sure you have the numbers available and as accurate as possible.

Step #2: Educational marketing.

The days of multimillion-dollar budgets for marketing using Super Bowl ads and digital billboards in Times Square are long behind us. While companies with big budgets can still utilize those avenues, you can stay competitive by simply providing content that educates as opposed to constantly trying to advertise your product or service. Focus on creating articles, videos, and other content that uses your expertise to educate people.

Action item: Focus on creating one piece of educational content per month and do three things with it: put it on your company blog, send it out to your email list, and make printed copies available to distribute when meeting with prospects and clients.

Step #3: Track your sales funnel.

In order to succeed in sales, you must always know how many prospects and leads you have in the various stages of your funnel. Most business owners make the mistake of thinking that the most important step in the sales process is getting orders. But research shows that this is the part of the sales process over which you have the least amount of control. Focus on tracking every step of your sales process, starting with the most important step of all, which is at the very top of your sales funnel. It typically includes making an initial contact of some sort or lead capture system.

Action item: Invest in a CRM solution that tracks your sales funnel or set up an Excel sheet where you track all of the stages within your sales process with exact numbers on a daily basis. One particular tool you can try is called Streak, a plug-in for Google Chrome that works directly in Gmail. I have found it to be an incredibly simple way of tracking sales funnels without the cumbersome aspects of a full CRM.

Step #4: Revolutionize your industry.

Stop trying to do what everyone else in your industry does. While it is critical that you adopt all of the best practices from within your industry, you cannot stop there. Focus on finding new ways of doing things that no one else is doing. Listen to your customers and focus on what you can do that others are simply not doing or unwilling to do. Steve Jobs did not attempt to make another flip phone or a Blackberry lookalike back in 2007; he absolutely revolutionized the mobile phone industry. No matter what kind of phone you carry today, remember that it's because of Steve Jobs that you have it.

Action item: Calendar a three-hour block once per month by yourself or with the most innovative members of your team, discussing what you could be doing that no one else in your industry does.

Step #5: Focus on solving your customers' pain points, not talking at them about what you do.

Most websites, brochures, and sales presentations focus on what a company provides. Set yourself apart by focusing instead on how you address your customers' pain points and how you can make their jobs and lives easier. Slowly change your presentations, website content, and brochures to come from the perspective of addressing customer pain points, instead of talking about yourself.

Action item: Take thirty minutes every two weeks to do an in-depth interview of one current client with the focus of understanding their jobs, their lives, and their businesses so you can identify their pain points. By the end of the year, you will have twenty-four different perspectives with an investment of only twelvehours of your time.

Step #6: Create standard operating procedures.

Functions within an organization that rely on an individual business owner or employee to do something just right are simply not scalable. To have a scalable business that allows you to grow consistently, you must create standard operating procedures for the most important functions. These procedures are step-by-step instructions for how something is to be done and they are stored in a centralized location. Consider a service such as SweetProcess to do this for you.

Action item: Take fifteenminutes per week to document one current process within your organization, and make sure that that procedure is put into action and used consistently starting the moment it is created.

Step #7: Focus on raving fan customer service.

Satisfied customers are useless in a world where we are so incredibly connected. Your organization's customer service goal should be to create a consistent stream of raving fans and those who are fanatical about what you do. Go above and beyond for every client in order to consistently create raving fan customers. Even the most dissatisfied, unhappy, and even angry customers can be turned into raving fans if they realize just how much you care about them and what they have to say.

Action item: Look up and find your worst online review and make it your mission to convert that individual into a raving fan within seven days or less. If your business does not have online reviews, reach out to the last client who was less than 100% satisfied.

Step #8: Build your company's social media presence.

Today, your company absolutely must have a social media presence in order for you to succeed. If you think that social media is just for fun or for the younger generation, you are missing out on the biggest opportunity to grow your available business today. Even if you only do B2B, understand that Google is now looking at social media engagement as a metric to see if you are relevant within your industry.

Action item: Ensure that your company has all of the following fan pages and you have daily (or at least weekly) posts on all of these platforms: Facebook, Twitter, LinkedIn, Instagram, Google +, and Pinterest. Even if each platform isn't right for your industry, it's worth having to boost your search engine optimization (SEO).

Step #9: Blog on your company's website.

Regardless of your industry, you must have a blog on your company website and ensure that you have a weekly post. If you are not a writer yourself and you don't think you have time for a weekly update, you can tap into employees, friends, and even customers for content. Additionally, while your ideal blog post would be 500 words or more, you can make simple blog posts that are no more than a paragraph and even things that you can copy and paste from an email that you wrote. The key is that the search engines want to see new content on your website and your customers will begin engaging with your content, even if you do not see the value. If you have no clue how to setup a blog, try a simple platform such as WordPress.

Action item: If you have a blog already, create a content calendar for the next twelvemonths. If you do not have a blog, start one today and make your first post by tomorrow.

Step #10: Know exactly who your ideal client is.

In an era where digital marketing platforms allow you to identify your target audience with every intricate detail, it is critical that you know exactly who your ideal client is. Whether you are B2B or B2C, you must know every detail of your ideal client, including demographics about company size, revenue, profits, age, gender, interests, and many other details. If you think that "anyone" can be your ideal client, you are essentially marketing to no one.

Action item: Use the Facebook Ads Manager tool to identify your ideal client today. While this is a tool created for those placing an ad on Facebook, you can use it easily as a tool to identify your target audience by spending five minutes selecting the various attributes of your ideal client and never placing the ad.

Step #11: Remind yourself WHY you are in your business.

Many entrepreneurs want to know howto succeed or whatthey need to do to succeed. Instead, the question is *why* do I do what I do? If you get connected with why you are in business, the "how" and the "what" will come much more easily. One easy way of figuring out why you are in business is to fastforward to a time when you have already achieved your goals and see what you enjoy the most about this victory.

Action item: Spend tenminutes today making a list of why you are in business and what your end goal is with what you do.

Step #12: Balance your life to become a great leader.

It may be hard to imagine that 80% of your organization's success is based on your mindset, as opposed to your products, services, marketing, and anything else you can imagine. Focus on getting yourself in a place where you are at your best, including balance in your life between health, wealth, relationships, and business, and enjoy how much easier business will become.

Action item: Take five minutes to rate your current status on the ten areas on the Titanium Wheel of Life. By giving yourself a score from 1 to 10 on each of these areas, you will quickly see where you may need to spend some time in order to have a smoother wheel that can roll along faster and better.

Step #13: Develop a KPI dashboard.

Every company, every department, and every position must have a key performance indicator (KPI) dashboard to track the most important measures on a regular basis. The best KPI dashboards have less than five items that are tracked on a daily, weekly, and monthly basis. By tracking these metrics, you will start to see where your focus needs to go. The result is that you and your team will begin to make massive headway in your business.

Action item: Think of the three to five most important numbers within your business that you can track on a daily basis. If you think of something that cannot be tracked as frequently, put that on a separate list.

Step #14: Work harder than your competitors.

Genius is simply a lifetime of effort put forth in private for just a few moments of seemingly effortless results in public. Don't be fooled by those who tell you that genetics, luck, and opportunity are the reasons for success. The most successful people in the world simply work harder than anyone else. Don't think you can beat your competitor if they are working while you are sleeping.

Action item: For one day, wake up two hours before you normally rise, even if that means waking up at 3:00 a.m. Get yourself ready and go to the office. On your way to the office, think about the fact that you are working while your competitors sleep. These next two hours are free time that you have in order to gain an edge over all of your competitors—notice how that makes you feel.

Step #15: If you have a family, kiss each of them every morning and every night.

For just a moment, I want to speak to you as a fellow entrepreneur. Throughout my life, I have worked harder than just about anyone else I've ever known. This has been the secret to my success. But one practice I started last year has given me a feeling like nothing else before it. If you are like me, sometimes you have no choice but to wake up before your spouse or kids and get home from work after they have already gone to sleep. Take two minutes each morning and night, going to each of their beds and just give them a little kiss. My two little girls and my beautiful princess certainly appreciate the little kisses I give then on my way out.

Action item: Do something to take care of your family today, not because you want to be a better husband, wife, father, or mother, but because your business coach, Arman Sadeghi, told you so.

These fifteenSteps are things that can help inject rocket fuel into your business, so do not take them lightly. Focus on applying as many of these as you possibly can and review this list often, even treating it as a monthly checklist. Finally, please share this list and this book with other entrepreneurs who can gain an edge from it.

Additional Resources

Titanium Live Event

See Arman Sadeghi Live!
Attend the world-class seminar that has been called "Part seminar and part rock concert!" and learn how to combine business and life in a way that will catapult you to the top and bring you lasting success and fulfillment. Arman teaches the science of success and the art of fulfillment in this incredible three-day event.
Check **www.titaniumsuccess.com/titanium-live** for more details including dates and locations.

Titanium Life App

Download the Titanium Life app on your iPhone or Android device for additional business tools and material.

Coaching

If you are looking to take your business or the executives in your business to a level like you've never imagined possible, consider enrolling for Arman's one-on-one coaching or executive coaching. There is a wait list in order to receive these services so if you are interested, be sure to book as early as possible.

Keynote Speaker

Arman speaks regularly at trade shows and company events.
Please go to **www.titaniumsuccess.com** or call **(844) 884-8264** for booking information.

(844) 884-8264
www.titaniumsuccess.com
facebook.com/titaniumsuccess
twitter.com/titaniumsuccess
youtube.com/titaniumsuccess
instagram.com/titaniumsuccess

TITANIUM
SUCCESS DOWN TO A SCIENCE